MW01251222

One is Still a Whole Number

A Christian Single's Successful Journey Continues

Gwendolyn J. Wheeler

INFINITY
PUBLISHING.COM

Copyright © 2009 by Gwendolyn J. Wheeler

ISBN 0-7414-5506-4

Published by:

INFIN ITY
PUBLISHING.COM

1094 New DeHaven Street, Suite 100
West Conshohocken, PA 19428-2713
Info@buybooksontheweb.com
www.buybooksontheweb.com
Toll-free (877) BUY BOOK
Local Phone (610) 941-9999
Fax (610) 941-9959

Printed in the United States of America

Published August 2009

Contents

Dedication

This book is dedicated to my wonderful mom, Beatrice Wheeler. She allowed me to live single comfortably longer in her home than most would have. You have always been my friend, strength, and oasis from the storms of life.

In 2005 our special relationship was changed when you had your first stroke. It changed even more when Dementia set in and you had your third stroke on July 4, 2008.

The hardest day of my life was when I realized I could no longer take care of you at home, and I had to commit you to the care of a nursing home. How my heart aches and I miss our close mother and daughter relationship. I have lost part of you that will never be recovered on this side of heaven. I love you so much, and I appreciate all the love and support you gave me throughout my life.

I smile as I think about how you told somebody recently I was like your mother. Yes, the daughter has now become the caretaker. We drive each other crazy because Dementia has you in another world I don't understand, and I keep trying to fix it. Poor me— I refuse to accept the fact that I can't fix this.

On the following page is a letter my mother wrote to me before she had her stroke in 2005.

A Letter from My Mother

August 23, 2005, 3:50 PM

Dearest Gwen:

My Dear Beloved daughter and pastor. Here I sit at my favorite spot in the house—the kitchen table. It is so hard to hold back the tears of joy as God brings back the memories of that cold night, January 28th in Joliet, Illinois. When I began to have pain, not too close to each other, I sensed it wouldn't be long before you would be entering into this world, so I decided to get up, do my laundry, and see that the house would be clean. Mother Brown, the Church Mother, had agreed to come to the house to care for the four small children I would be leaving at home. Your father was already prepared to pick her up.

So early on the morning of January 29, 1954, your father and I journeyed to the hospital. Soon after I was prepped, you, my miracle baby was born. You see we didn't know what all God had for you to do, but Satan knew you were a person of destiny. That was why he wanted to destroy you while you were still in my womb, but God intervened.

Look at you today—a two time author, an ordained elder, a pastor, and the most important thing you are a saved, anointed woman of God. I want you to know I am so proud of you. It has been a pleasure watching you grow from one level to the next. I want you to know I may not say it every day, but I love you very, very much and thank you for all you have done for me. A lot of places I would not have been able to go. A lot of things I could not have done. So congratulations on your new book, <u>On the Road to Recovery Again...</u> I am praying that many people will be saved and healed. Love you, your Mother B. Wheeler

Introduction

"Lord, I don't want to be alone." Those words were spoken one night as I stood behind our family's car. I was 14 years old, newly born again, and had just broken up with my first official boyfriend. The reason for the break-up was because I was told that now that I was a Christian I could not have an unsaved boyfriend. That concerned me because even at that young age I knew there were few Christian males in the church.

Why was a 14 year old girl worried about being alone? My whole life was ahead of me, and finding a mate should have been the last thing on my mind. Finding out who I was should have been utmost in my mind. Furthermore, educational choices, traveling, career paths, and just enjoying being a teenager should have been occupying my mind.

Where were the life coaches—the cheerleaders for young ladies emerging into womanhood? Back then there was no such thing—young ladies were expected to be wives and mothers. A career was something to do while you were waiting for the main event—marriage.

Thankfully, although I didn't have a human life coach, my heavenly Father was in fact my life coach, working out the affairs in my life. Many times I came along kicking and screaming—this isn't the way I want my life to go.

Through every painful event in my life I have become stronger. That hasn't been an automatic result. I am constantly struggling to remember to lay everything at the foot of the cross and just rest in God. He is able to handle everything better than I. I must believe the words written on my cup: *"Good morning, this is God! I will be handling all your problems today. I will not need your help—so have a good day. I love you!"*

One Is Still A Whole Number (A Christian Single's Successful Journey Continues) is the title of this 14th anniversary edition of One is A Whole Number.

The title was changed to reflect the fact that some years have passed, and my life has changed.

So much has happened since 1995 when I published the first edition of, One is A Whole Number (Successful Single Living from a Christian's Perspective). Yet my conclusion remains the same—you can be happy and whole as a single person.

Chapter One

Celebrate Life—Celebrate Where You Are and Where You Are Going!

Today I celebrate my life—the life that God so graciously gave to me. The life He continues to sustain and fulfills for me. He continues to be my Father, my Creator and my Best Friend. Before I came out of my mom's womb, He was with me and has been the unseen Presence in my life that kept life's tragedies from killing me.

My single years are to be commemorated. Yes, I have had my struggles: the loneliness, the sexual temptations (some fiercer than others), the desperation, the wrong choices, betrayals, failures, rejections, heartbreak/heartache, and the "wrong man syndrome". Certainly, I have asked the question, why am I still single, God? That has haunted me, but not for long. God has always comforted me.

Mid-life is here—no place for regrets or self-pity. I am here now. Fifty-five—how did I reach this age so soon? With midlife come changes in my health—high blood pressure, less energy, aches and pains in every part of my body. The body doesn't work like it used to, but thank God I am alive. Every day I wake up and can get up out of bed is a reason to celebrate.

Can a single woman embrace mid-life with grace? Yes, she can! With grace come appreciation, celebration, anticipation, and a great sense of humor. Early Retirement came on January 31, 2009. Yeah! I officially became a senior citizen on January 29th. Yes, I am a proud carrier of my AARP card and gladly accept any senior citizen discounts offered to me.

Retirement for me doesn't mean sitting in an easy chair. It means continuing on my path to destiny. I have a church to pastor, books to write and a new business, Sensational Floral Designs By Gwendolyn, to grow. Also, I need to upgrade my personal ministry business, Gwen Wheeler International Ministries, Inc.

I didn't reach this place by accident, but by divine appointment. If you read my book, <u>On the Road to Recovery Again...</u>, you know that if Satan had his way, my birth would not have occurred. His will didn't prevail—praise God! The will of God prevailed, so into this world was born a baby girl destined to do great things for God.

You have had your struggles, too, whether you are young, old, or in-between. There are some heart-wrenching stories of survival you can share. So let's pull out the party hats, the food, and the music and celebrate that none of these things have destroyed us. Instead they have enriched and made us stronger. In fact, you are looking good, better than you have ever looked before.

Struggles affect each of us differently. They assisted me in removing the clutters from life and discovering what is real and necessary. Their presence caused me to learn, grow, and become a God-dependent woman of excellence.

At fifty-five I am more fulfilled than I have ever been in my life. I am not merely a survivor, but I am contributor to life. Many gifts I provide as a pastor, evangelist, a counselor, published author, poet, visionary, trailblazer, daughter, a sister, a friend, aunt, entrepreneur, and successful business woman. These are major life accomplishments for a single woman.

Yet I am still on a journey to my greater place of destiny—my enlarged territory and fulfilled prophecies. This journey requires a lot of patience, stamina, flexibility, reevaluation, and rediscovery. Listening and listening again—relearning what I thought I knew. Rewriting the vision is part of the course mixed with setbacks, delays, heartaches and heartbreaks. Persevering through physical and emotional pain while walking through overwhelming and exhausting situations are to be expected. There are days when God's way seems too long and painful. The nights never seem to end. My perspective is limited, but God sees what is on the other side of the pain and it is marvelous.

Never settle for a life of mediocrity—the average life. Your life will be filled with frustration as you are haunted by your unfilled dreams and incomplete destiny. You'll make it to heaven, but you will never realize what life could have been like if you had only stuck it out.

My friends, there is so much inside of you that God wants to bring out of you while you are single. Find out what you want to do and do it! Take some classes, seminars, or workshops. Do your homework. Before I ever wrote one book I did my research. My first book did not turn out the way I wanted it to, but it was a start. Since then I have developed my skills better by attending classes and reading other books about writing, proofreading, and editing. My goal is to become a better writer with each book that I write. Patience is your greatest virtue. I tell myself that God didn't have me write books, so that they could just collect dust on my shelf. When the timing is right for me to emerge more into the world market, my books are ready to be shipped.

I have non-profit organizations that I started from scratch—all three have different Mission Statements with Bylaws and bank accounts. Understand this—before they became a reality, they were a thought. Then that thought was written down, and then a plan was developed and launched.

Don't sit around dreaming about Mr. Right coming to rescue you from your humdrum life. Get up and do something. If you are my age, you really need to get up and stop making excuses and apologies. Make a plan and take steps toward bettering your life. No, you are not satisfied where you are. I don't buy that. Don't let fear or a "stuck in the rut" attitude prevent you from becoming a person of excellence. There is a business, play, song, book, adventure, new career, and trip to a far away country inside of you. What are you going to do about it? Do some research; pick up the phone and call somebody.

Want a house? Didn't ask you what your economical situation is. There are so many programs available for first home buyers. Yes, I know the economy is in disaster, but what does that have to do with the God? He continuously does exceedingly abundantly above what we can ask or think. Everybody will not be fortunate to inherit property, but God will allow you to buy one. This is a faith walk, but Scripture says faith without works is dead or void. If you want to arrive at that dream destination, there are some things you must do yourself. Had some setbacks and disappointments lately? Don't quit.

One of my plaques is entitled *"Don't Quit"*. It has been adapted from the original poem. The words are:

When Things Go Wrong As They Sometimes Will,

When The Road You're Trudging Seems All Up Hill,

When You're Feeling Low And The Stress Is High,

And You Want To Smile But Have To Sigh,

When Worries Are Getting You Down A Bit...

By All Means Pray-And Don't You Quit.

Success Is Failure Turned Inside Out,

God's Hidden Gift In The Clouds Of Doubt.

You Never Can Tell How Close You Are-

It May Be Near When It Seems So Far.

So Trust In The Lord When You're Hardest Hit...

It's When Things Go Wrong That You Must Not Quit!

Stay in the race, live life to the fullest, and celebrate. Celebrate the fact that you are still alive and that every day presents you with another opportunity to experience all the things God has prepared for you.

Life will not always make sense to us, but when God is guiding our lives, you can celebrate and be at peace knowing God is faithful. In His own time He will work out the greater purpose for your life. He does not provide us a step by step manual that will provide us with explanations of why we are where we are or why we are going through what we are going through. Instead He says trust Me. I know what I am doing.

The problem with most of us, including myself, is that we are so busy trying to get to the larger place of destiny that we fail to see all the smaller miracles God has planted along the way to encourage and inspire us. True celebration is when we can celebrate while we are in the process/preparation/journey.

Destiny's process is like going on a trip by plane. There are usually stopovers—some longer than others. Sometimes you have to run across the airport in order to make your connections. Other times you have time to have dinner. Then there are the times the weather makes it necessary to spend the night in a hotel at the airport. This is not where you are going, but it is a necessary stop along the way. These stopovers are often orchestrated by God, but we are so busy complaining that we miss the fact that God has provided us an opportunity to rest, regroup and hear His voice. Most times we are moving too rapidly to hear Him speak. We miss the opportunity to get answers to our prayers, receive new assignments and creative ideas.

Furthermore, I believe God wants us to learn the blessedness of contentment in whatever season we are in. Every season has it twists and turns—bitters and sweets. But He doesn't want us to be twisted and bitter. Contentment is one of our greatest assets. Don't allow the circumstances of life to control you. Walk in perpetual peace regardless of what is happening. Because of Who God is, walk in joy. Nothing has to change or be gained—we can celebrate—rejoice here and now.

Learning to be content is a life-long lesson. Every new assignment demands us to grow more. When God shows us the vision of our greater destiny, He doesn't usually show us the process that has been designed by Him to make us tailor-made for that place. Sometimes there are a lot of dark places we must walk through first: the heartaches, loneliness, pain (physical and mental), emotional, rejection, betrayals, delays, loss of faith, loss of friends, and loss of things. If you knew that in advance, you might say, never mind God, I'll settle for mediocrity.

For some of us mediocrity is never an option. God has put such a strong fire and passion within us that mediocrity would be more painful than the other trials. Others can't understand what seems from the outside to be a strong, unwavering drive to be and achieve. In reality it is a strong inner spiritual hunger that can only be satisfied as we are fulfilling the plan of God for our lives.

The lesson of contentment is a class I have failed so often. I desire so much to be in my larger place of destiny. It's such a struggle for me to live in this in-between place, where I experience so many frustrations. Yet true faith means walking in peace and joy—not misery—as you walk in the in-between places of your life.

Just in case you do not understand my dilemma with my in-between place, let me explain what it is. An in-between place is when you are working a full-time job while trying to grow your home business on the side. Your passion and heart is in your home business, which is your life-long dream. This place is where you experience happiness and contentment. Although your clientele has grown considerably since you began, it hasn't grown enough to pay the bills.

There are nights and weekends you have to put many hours and much energy into your home business. Understandably you are running on empty and you are exhausted. The alarm clock goes off too soon on Monday morning. You struggle to get of bed to go to a job that bores and frustrates you. But the bills have to be paid and you have to eat, my friend. So off to the work you go with coffee in hand. That's an in-between place.

Learning important lessons is another reason to celebrate. There are so many of them. Learn this one: In-between places are not wasted places. They are places that teach us lessons we could never learn anywhere else. While working for someone else, we learn to be trustworthy, committed, and our skills are honed. All these things are considered "transferable" skills; we will need them in order to fulfill our dreams.

Being content in the in-between place, while walking to the place of destiny, is quite a balancing act. They seem to overlap at times. Before I retired, and sometimes even now, burnt-out knocked at my door, threatening to beat me down. Some days I handle it well and some days I don't. I went through a period when I thought I can't take this anymore and asked family and friends to pray for my release into my full destiny. Weariness overwhelmed me to the point that I cried out, "God, You know how tired I am." Along with this weariness I had an on-going battle with Vertigo (a spinning in my head). Went to a specialist and he said he was confused, because I didn't show any physical signs of it in my eyes. MRI was ordered and praise God there were no signs of physical abnormalities.

My personal prescription for this bout with Vertigo would be long days of sweet solitude and rest. This would revive and restore me. No schedules, no tasks to compete or projects to finish—just a date with rest and relaxation. I can hear them calling my name.

While the voices of R&R beckons me to come, the Voice of One who knows me well and holds and guides my future speaks louder. I hear Him saying, "Gwen, rest is necessary not only for the body and mind, but also for the soul. You are tired because of all the things that are on your plate, but I want you to enter a spiritual rest. This rest is not dependent or controlled by outward, temporary circumstances. Circumstances come and go, but my rest is available all the time through every season and circumstance. Hear the words of My Son, "Come unto Me all ye that labor and are heavy laden and I will give you rest."

The labor we must rest from is the kind that we do while relying on our own strength and wisdom. We could accomplish more in a shorter period of time if we go in the strength of the Lord. The strength and wisdom He gives us won't be distracted by all the things that happen within our lives.

So let's celebrate another lesson we have learned. When you are feeling blue, and celebrating doesn't seem an easy thing to do, make yourself sing. Some days your best song might be Hallelujah anyhow. Never let the devil get you down. When old Satan comes your way, hold your head up high and say, hallelujah anyhow. There will be plenty of Hallelujah anyhow days. Our hearts will know both joy and sadness. Regardless of what life brings to our door today, let's celebrate! Take a trip, go to a spa (get a massage and a facial), take yourself out to dinner, or just crawl up in the bed with a good book or watch an old-time movie. Just relax, rejuvenate, and pamper yourself. Celebrate!

Chapter Two

Over Fifty and Loving It
(Insight, Inspiration, Lessons, and Wisdom)

Turning fifty is a milestone in one's life—it is a time of reflection. You think about where you've been and where you are going. Joys and sorrows have been my life's companions—both have been teachers who have taught me the importance of celebrating life's survival.

I thought it might be sort of fun and interesting to compare how I felt about certain issues when I was forty and how I feel about them now at fifty-five. Here are the comparisons:

Birthdays

• Forty—I turned forty on January 29, 1994. I admit at first I was apprehensive about turning forty. As a single person I was not sure of how I would handle it or how I would feel. To my surprise, it was the best birthday I ever had. I told people I didn't know turning forty could be so much fun. My whole family was there to celebrate and I was grateful.

• Fifty—I turned fifty on January 29, 2004. I embraced that birthday with so much joy and anticipation—no apprehension whatsoever. I had so many reasons to celebrate. My family and friends gave me a wonderful birthday party. It was held in the fellowship hall of the church I held services at. My brother, Herman, said when he turned fifty I asked him how it felt. He then asked me how it felt. It felt great. My life had drastically changed since my 40th birthday— two of my brothers and my grandmother passed away. I was Assistant Pastor then, but now a Pastor of a church I birthed and a published author of 3 books and four more are waiting to be completed. I am a entrepreneur, who has launched the business of her dreams, Sensational Floral Designs By Gwendolyn. In spite of everything my family and I have gone through, God has been good to us. Opening my church was the beginning of my walk into my destiny with so much more ahead of me.

Aging

• Forty- I think I have a lot more aches and pain. My energy level has certainly changed. My doctor would attribute that to lack of exercise and not eating the right foods. People keep telling me I don't look forty. Of course, I don't know what forty is supposed to look like. I do know I concentrate a lot more on preventing the aging process and spend more money on creams for my face than I used to spend. How much more gray hair do I have? I haven't decided. Trips are made to the salon occasionally and the attendants rinse the gray away.

• Fifty—I don't really think a lot about aging as far as the physical changes. Although when I look in the mirror, I think I am aging well. Except this last year I have just gained too much weight. There has been a lot of stress because of having to deal with my mom's health and affairs. I have eaten too much comfort food, and I don't like what I see when I look in the mirror or see my pictures, especially the full length ones. Sorry, I don't feel like singing the theme song for being a big girl—Big and Beautiful. I need to take this weight off. I still love myself, but I would feel better after I take some pounds off. Everyone has to find their comfort zone and I have passed mine. Getting depressed won't solve anything, but using my YMCA membership card will. So off to the gym I am going, and I live near the beach, so it is time to put on the sneakers and start walking again.

Don't think I have any more pains than I had when I was in my forties. Stiffness is due to my inactivity. Won't go over that subject again. How much more gray hair do I have? Too much! It grows in real fast and it is becoming more and more resistant to rinses, but I won't let it win. I am not ready to give into the gray. Trips are still made to the salon occasionally or I do it myself.

Before April 2008 I wrote: What has changed is the level of stress that I have to deal with—that affects how I feel. I am just looking forward to the day when I can officially retire from Corporate America. Looking forward to being a healthy senior citizen. The daily commute tires me out; I want to be able to sit on my retirement patio in the morning and drink my coffee and work in my garden.

Update: While waiting to finish this book, I retired. No more daily commute to work, but I am still tired. So many things still to be done. Being a person of destiny requires a lot of energy and the ability to organize and balance your time and projects. I need help in those areas.

Marriage

• Forty—After going through my tremendous heartbreak, I fluctuated on whether I wanted to get married. When someone asked me when I was going to get married, I shocked them and said, "If I get married I do, if I don't I don't, but I am going to live."

There is life outside of marriage, and you can really be happy. I was at peace and I was not going to be a desperate single woman. Society's view was not going to govern my life—didn't look at myself as being an "old maid" or "spinster", but instead I looked at myself as being a single woman who had learned that real satisfaction and joy come from having a right relationship with God. God's grace got me through those difficult days when I wrestled with my singleness.

- Fifty—At 55 I still believe I will get married, but yet the thought scares me at times. In recent years I have seen strong, powerful, successful women broken because of failed marriages. I want to be married to someone who loves me enough to support me through every season of my life. He has to understand that I am a woman of destiny and I am called to be successful. I have worked and prayed too hard to get this far, and I do not want to have to choose between my destiny and a husband. I will support him — most women automatically will support their husbands. But support should be a mutual gift.

There are too many women who do not have my calling, and rather than trying to change me, he can go find another woman. Does that sound cold? I personally don't think women should have to make that decision, but unfortunately they do. In my early twenties I was told that if some men saw me sitting on the platform they might not want to marry me. My radical response was marriage is not my main objective. He was shocked, and I was pleased that I was able to say and mean that. I still mean that.

The prophecy I got in 1988 was that my husband would be tailor-made. I guess because of my complexity this has been a long process. Well at this point it doesn't make sense to fret about it; I will just continue to trust God.

Having Children

- Forty—My maternal instinct was satisfied through being a Godmother, an aunt, and a great aunt. In 2000 the issue was settled forever when I had a hysterectomy. You'll have to read about that in my book, <u>On the Road to Recovery Again...</u>

- Fifty—Needless to say, that is not even a subject that needs to be discussed anymore. I am very much satisfied with birthing spiritual babies.

Having Roots/My Own Home

- Forty—I believe that singles should make investments into permanency. Everybody may not be able to afford a home right now, but hopefully you plan to in the future. In the meantime, you can make the place you live in a lot more comfortable. Doesn't take a lot of money—just be creative and put things within it that express your personality and taste. It doesn't matter if you live in an apartment or room; make it look like you live there.

It was my plan to be in my own place by forty, and I told my mother years ago if I wasn't married by forty I was getting my own place. In the midst of my plans God spoke and said not yet. Didn't give me a reason at first, but then made it plain it was time to buy another car. Years later the reason became more apparent.

- Fifty—I became a homeowner when my mother transferred the ownership of our family home to me. All my brothers and sisters were in agreement. It felt good to actually say my mother lives with me instead of the opposite. Besides at eighty she really didn't need to worry about the care of a home. God actually knew what was ahead; my mother was not going to be able to take care of the household responsibilities. She had a stroke that same year. By the grace of God she was able to recover at home for a while, but as I stated in the beginning of this book she had a couple of more strokes in 2008. Unfortunately, her physical and mental health kept declining and I had to commit her to the care of a nursing home.

My home is not a mansion, but it is my home. It is peaceful and comfortable —a place that I can entertain in. God has allowed me to make much needed renovations that make it a more pleasant place to live. God is faithful and He does answer prayers.

Finances

• Forty—Some folks think single folks automatically should have a good financial status, but we overspend just like married people. We need to budget our money, because our finances are capable of being out of whack like anybody else's. It is not how much you make, but how well you manage it. Therefore, singles need to have a financial plan; you can do more than what you think you are capable of doing. You may have some setbacks along the way, but you will recover. Trust God and give to Him what is rightfully His, and then you know you can depend on Him to bring you not only out of financial dilemmas, but He will bring an increase into your life. I don't believe we have to struggle all of our lives. We need to remember who our Source of Supply is and don't let becoming rich be your main goal. Keep God as the focus of your affections and priority, and He will help you to recover from those financial problems you have been through. Nothing is ever a hopeless case when God is in the plan.

My focus then was to pay off bills, save money, and have good credit—I was doing pretty well for a while. Strayed somewhat from my plan.

• Fifty—My focus is still to pay off bills, save money, and have good credit. But life has changed since I was in my forties. Retirement was twenty years away then, but now at 55 I am retired, but early retirement means a smaller pension and I can't collect social security until about 7 years from now. I am a pastor and have a couple of businesses and books, but they haven't taken off like I need them to, so I must manage my spending. Above all of that, God continues to be my greatest Financial Resource. On the day that I was installed as pastor we marched into the tune of Bless me indeed—increase my territory. My wealthy place is being prepared for me, and the God who does exceedingly abundantly above all I can ask or think is in charge of that project.

Concluding Reflections

My conclusion for my life at forty is summed up in the poem below.

TURNING FORTY

By Gwendolyn J. Wheeler

It's hard to believe I turned 40 two years ago;

A lot has happened since then that has made me grow.

I celebrated that day when I turned forty,

With family and friends at my birthday party.

No regrets or disappointments were felt in any way,

Just joy, love and gratitude on that special day.

The year before had been such a devastating one,

And I was glad when it was over and done.

I entered a new decade with new and special dreams,

With a determination to keep a healthy self-esteem.

I felt renewed vigor and cherished my dignity,

And I'm trusting in God to fulfill my destiny.

A stronger woman emerged out of the painful ashes,

Ashes filled with heartaches and many of life's clashes.

I celebrate the fact that I have survived,

And I am praising God for being wonderfully alive.

I am more confident now than I have ever been before,

God will go ahead of me and open up every door.

Forty in the Bible was a monumental age;

People became heroes and emerged from every page.

Visions which once seemed impossible to achieve,

Were suddenly realized by those who dared to believe.

They believed the promises God had made in the past,

And sorrow was turned into joy at last.

So forty is my time to be abundantly blessed,

For I have been faithful and passed every test.

Standing at the threshold of a miraculous tomorrow,

I am saying good-bye to disappointments and sorrow.

Fifty Reflections

Didn't write a poem about turning fifty, but just want to say it is good to be fifty-five—I am loving it. Don't know how many years of single living I have left, but I plan to be successful through the duration, and then I will take that success into my married life. Someone may ask is life the way you dreamed it would be at 50. My answer is I never thought about what life would be at fifty. I guess I just crossed over without much thought.

My single friends, whatever age you are at, please just make every effort to enjoy life. We all have problems and difficult days to walk through, but God is walking through them with you. You are going to be just fine. I talk more about marriage in the fourth chapter, so read on.

My final reflection in this chapter is about a prophecy I received in 1985. Here's the prophecy...

"No event, no incident, no person in your life is by chance or accident. God has been forming a pattern and when He is finished, you'll be able to look back and it will all make sense. God's hand is on your life."

• My editorial on the above prophecy at 40 was this:

So you may ask the question, are things adding up in your life? Can you see a pattern? Is anything making sense? My answer to all those questions is yes!

God allowed the pain in my life to serve as a crucible to burn away my tendency to rely on other people. I have often relied on other people to be what only He could be in my life. For God is my everlasting Source of life, love, peace, joy, satisfaction, provision and contentment. There is no one who can compete with Him. All the negative and painful places I walked through were the vehicles He used to get my attention. He wanted me to desire to know and love Him more than anybody else.

All my mistakes, struggles and failures are constant reminders that I am what I am by the grace of God. Every time I am broken by hurts, disappointments, or rejection, it is another opportunity for the fragrance of Christ to pour out of my life. It is another opportunity for me to decrease and Christ to increase.

• This wise woman of 55 wrote a shorter perception of the above prophecy:

The pattern God formed in my life is a beautiful tapestry of grace and glory woven through pain and sorrow. Each difficult stitch made me into a God-dependent woman of excellence. They evolved me into a woman who would become a life coach for others—a cheerleader for those who lack the passion to pursue all that life has to offer them.

It is such a great feeling to know that my life is not over at 55. In fact, my whole life is before me, and I can hardly wait to experience all the blessings and places of destiny that God has prepared for me.

Chapter Three

I am Single—I am Whole

When I first began to write about wholeness in 1989, my perception was very different than what it is today. In fact, I felt at the age of 35 I was finally living as a whole woman. I was no longer the young girl who felt she needed a man to make her complete. By the grace of God I survived some heartache that could have destroyed me. I felt stronger and more confident in who I was.

Then at the age of 39 I experienced a heartbreak that shattered my whole life—that heartbreak is discussed in Chapter 7. As I fought to regain my life, I discovered a new sense of wholeness. This wholeness comes only after you have gone through great pain and brokenness and have been healed by the Lord Jesus Christ. He continues to be the Great Physician.

True wholeness involves a healing that occurs first on the inside, and then it flows out of you. When you are healed inwardly, it affects how you respond to the rest of the world around you. Without inward healing you can become bitter, resentful, unforgiving, insensitive, indifferent, skeptical, forlorn, untrusting and aloof.

Yes, even a Christian can experience the above negative emotions. The effects of some of the things you go through are like being in a tragic car accident. If by God's grace you survive, you must go through a period of rehabilitation. To rehabilitate a person means to restore them to useful life through education and therapy. You have to learn how to walk, live, and trust the voice of God again. Rehabilitation is a process that requires a lot of patience and determination.

Time alone will not bring about healing because it is what you do within time that determines whether you will be healed. Here are some suggestions:

➤ Surround yourself with Godly, praying people who will carry you in prayer. You need people who will love you enough to intercede for you through the nights of your life until the sun shines again.

➤ Pray yourself. Lofty and melodious words are not required. Fragmented sentences are accepted, and phrases without a subject or a verb can be understood by God. You can be honest in prayer

➤ Read and meditate on the Word of God, especially the book of Psalms. Whatever you are experiencing right now has been experienced by others in the Bible who survived. Their testimony can help you.

Read books by Christian authors who have gone through similar experiences. I thank God for these men and women of God. They will never know how much they helped me during the time in my life when I was in the "Intensive Care Unit". These authors were the spiritual doctors and nurses who provided blood transfusion and antibiotics that helped me through my depressing time. I experienced a new sense of wholeness—being healed from the inside out—because of what they wrote.

Wholeness also means: finished, complete, abun-dantly supplied, equipped, sound, healthy, restored and healed. People, especially women, are constantly struggling to find out who they are and what they need in their lives in order to become a whole person. When

God created all of us, He made us complete or whole. Nothing was needed.

For many years singles were made to believe that wholeness could be obtained only through marriage. We misunderstood the words written in Matthew 19:4-6 which says:

"And He answered and said to them, "Have you not read that He who made them at the beginning 'made them male and female,' and said, 'For this reason a man shall leave his father and mother and be joined to his wife, and the two shall become one flesh'? So then, they are no longer two but one flesh. Therefore what God has joined together, let not man separate."

People felt the word, one, represented the numeral, 1, which stands for a whole unit in mathematics. Somehow they concluded since two people would make one in marriage, then apart from each other they were a half person. Yet the oneness God spoke about here is the unity and harmony that should exist within marriage.

God does not make half people who have to search their whole lives to find their missing part. He created us whole beings. We are a gift by ourselves and have something to contribute to life.

Singles suffer from the "half person" syndrome, especially single women. Their lives are placed on hold while they search for Mr. Right. They hope to be happy when that special person comes. However, there is no guarantee they will come and if they do come, why should you waste all those years of singleness in sadness and gloom. Today is the day to be happy. Enjoy the life that God has given you now! Jesus said in John 10:10, "I have come that they may have life, and that they may have it more abundantly."

Abundant living is not dependent on your marital status, but has to do with our relationship with Christ. It is time for us to be healed from the "half person" syndrome. Be all you can be for the Master now, and don't put off for tomorrow what you can be today—a whole person.

For many years I suffered from the "half person" syndrome. As I was preparing to leave high school, I did not set any solo goals for successful living. Having a career or doing anything that would better my life did not occur to me. Those objectives would be temporary because I was going to get married and have children. I believed the factors of wholeness were love, peace, joy, contentment, and real satisfaction. It didn't seem possible that I could experience these factors while being single, so marriage had to be my pivotal goal. So like many other singles I set out on a life-long journey to find this wonderful person who would complete my life and make me whole.

My journey to find Mr. Right and at the same time find wholeness has been long and painful. I have suffered many heartaches, disappointments and rejection. My heart has been filled with loneliness and despair as I sat through weddings. As I watched others get married before me, I wondered and questioned God about when my turn would come. My dream of finding true happiness was always dependent on my getting married. I didn't believe it was possible to live a truly happy and whole life without a husband.

A year after high school I met someone I thought I was going to marry, so I purchased my first set of china on an installment plan. That first purchase was to be the beginning of many years of buying things for the future. When I did not get married at the age of 19, I just kept looking and hoping that Mr. Right would arrive. I spent many hours depressed about being single. This pain was soothed by purchasing things for my future house. Everything you could imagine was bought: china, crystal, silverware, pots and pans, pictures, Tupperware, etc.

There were days when I didn't look forward to going home. I didn't have a husband waiting there to love me and make my life worthwhile. Those words now bring a smile to my face and laughter from my heart. My perception on life has changed and grown greatly. I enjoy single life and can go into a restaurant by myself, order a meal, and enjoy it without making any apologies. My solitude is greatly appreciated.

The above contentment came about at a great price—I made some very painful mistakes. For example, the person I thought I wanted to marry at 19 came back into view when I was 30. All signs seemed to point towards us becoming a married couple. Unfortunately, I approached this situation in the wrong way. My memory is somewhat cloudy, but I do remember I told him that I felt we were to get married. I wrote him a letter and called him.

After two years of waiting and believing we would be married, my dream exploded in my face and left me reeling from side to side. He chose to marry someone else. This was a great disappointment. I felt humiliated, angry, hurt, betrayed, and couldn't understand what happened. Yet I had to pick up the pieces and go on.

Hindsight teaches us a lot and I shared what I learned in that particular situation in Chapter 6. For your convenience I will repeat it in this chapter which is as follows:

"God's design for marriage is that man is to be the pursuer and woman the pursued. I don't believe that there is only one person you can be married to—God gives us options. Both wills have to line

up with each other. As you will agree, typically men have more options than women do. Sometimes he may be praying about two available options. You may be the better choice, but because you made the first move, he decided on the other option. There is something within a normal man's makeup that says I want to make the first move. Don't get angry with God because He didn't make this man marry you. Accept the fact that you violated the rules and nullified the plans. So move on."

Through this painful lesson God taught me the importance of letting go of past hurts and disappointments. He taught me a powerful truth through the illustration of a caterpillar's metamorphosis into a butterfly. A caterpillar is an ugly, hairy worm that crawls on the ground. Sometimes they are stepped on by humans. It is hard to think of this ugly insect becoming anything of beauty. Yet when the time is right, a caterpillar spins a cocoon. When the appropriate time has passed, it emerges from its cocoon as a beautiful butterfly. The beautiful colors are admired by all. In its new state as a butterfly, it can fly to higher ground because of the wings it now has.

So it is true within our Christian lives. Sometimes because of what we have done or others have done to us we feel ugly. We feel like we are crawling, and that we'll never gain any heights. Yet when we commit our lives to the Lord on a daily basis, He will turn us into something of beauty. God will give us spiritual wings that will enable us to rise about the things that once caused us to crawl and stumble. We will become useable, brand new, have a better testimony, and live a more joyful life.

This change calls for patience. Isaiah 40:31 tells us:

"But those who wait on the Lord shall renew their strength; They shall mount up with wings as eagles,

They shall run and not be weary, they shall walk and not faint."

The Prophet Isaiah further wrote in Isaiah 64:4:

"For since the beginning of the world men have not heard nor perceived by the ear, Nor has the eyes seen any God besides you, who acts for the one who waits for Him."

That painful season created a new and improved me, and I am truly grateful. God did not allow me to become hard or bitter. In fact, I highly respect the man I felt I was to marry. That's grace; that's God. Only He can allow you to love and forgive when you feel that you have been wronged or received the raw end of a deal.

As a result of this disappointment, I walked into my bedroom one day and looked at the boxes that were stacked up. They should have been marked "Future happiness". I took the things out of the boxes and began to use them. There were shelves, and pictures that I hung around my room. The decision made that day was to take my life off hold. I would no longer wait for Mr. Right to come, but I was going to live a full life now. Thank God I made that decision since I am still single at 55.

Over the years sometimes my life has felt too full. There were days I wondered what I would do if I had to add one more person to my already full schedule.

Where you are today is not an accident. You may be surprised but God is not. All the negative and positive circumstances that surround your life are meant to be instruments or pottery tools for God to make you better and stronger. Your ability to be the best is not dependent on your finding Mr. or Miss Right. Instead the emerging best you is dependent on your willingness to shed all the excuses. Allow God to make you a new, better person today!

In the 5th chapter of John we are given an account of a man who had been afflicted with an infirmity for 38 years. It is recorded that during a certain feast an angel would come and trouble the water of a pool called Bethesda. Whoever would step in the water first would be healed.

One day Jesus saw this man lying there and asked him a simple question, which required a simple answer. The question was "Wilt thou be made whole?" Rather than saying yes or no, the man replied, "Sir, I have no man, when the water is troubled to put me into the pool; but while I am coming, another steppeth down before me." Yet Jesus knew the man wanted to be whole, and so healed him by speaking the words, "Rise, take up thy bed, and walk." (KJV)

I love that portion of Scripture. I remember hearing a sermon preached from that passage entitled "You Can Walk." That message helped me to realize that even though emotionally I was temporarily crippled I did not have to remain that way. Jesus was speaking personally to me, "Gwen, you can walk!"

The greatest healing needed by this man was recorded in the 5th chapter of John—inward healing. Can you imagine all those years he spent feeling worthless and inadequate? In one instance Jesus changed all of that and made him whole inside and out.

So many people like this man have been confronted by Jesus and have been asked the same question, "Will you be made whole?" Like this man they blame other people for their inadequacies and disadvantages. Singles blame other people for their singleness. The gifts and talents within us lie dormant, and we don't live our life fully because we are single.

Sometimes their feelings of incompleteness stem from past hurts and rejections. Your heart may have been broken so many times that you feel like the nursery rhyme character, Humpty Dumpty. You feel no one can put you back together again.

The words of one of my favorite songs have comforted me during times of great pain and brokenness. They are: "A Potter saw a vessel that had been broken in the wind and the rain. He tried with so much compassion to put it together again. I was that broken vessel that no one thought was any good. Jesus picked up the pieces of my broken heart and revived my soul again."

We live in a broken world with broken lives, broken hearts and broken dreams. Being a Christian does not give us immunity from pain. There are circumstances and situations that have caused people to become broken and fractured human beings.

You may be one of those fractured people, and feel that no one cares. Too many times you have tried in vain to mend the pieces of your broken life filled with pain. The good news I want to share with you is that you are not alone. God cares about what you are going through or have been through. We all have fractures in our lives. Jesus is a healer of broken lives. He will not merely put cement into the cracks of your life, but He will make you brand new.

Let's pray this prayer together:

Father, I have been waiting for a human person to make me whole. Today I lay my life before you and ask that You heal me and make me whole. I surrender my past, my present, and future into Your hands. This day I stir up all the gifts within me and take my life off hold. By Your grace and with Your strength I will live a new life as a whole person! If I should forget my commitment today, please bring these words back to me. I want to experience the joy, peace and contentment that only a whole person can experience.

All these things I ask in the Name of Jesus Christ, Who died and rose from the grave so that I could be a whole person. Amen.

You are unique, and you are special. God believes in you, and now you must believe in yourself. Watch your life transform into something beautiful—a whole person. I will close this chapter with a poem I wrote regarding wholeness.

NEED FOR WHOLENESS

By Gwendolyn J. Wheeler

Empty places, shattered dreams, broken pieces that won't fit,

A need for companionship, a desire to be whole and not a misfit.

Trying to understand who I am and where I am going,

And what can soothe me and satisfy my deep longing.

Dreams of belonging to someone keep filling my mind,

Hoping that through this person completeness I'll find.

Completeness would mean love, peace, children, and a home,

Satisfaction, contentment, and a special place of my own.

For years I waited for my dreams of wholeness to come true,

While being disappointed, frustrated and ever so blue.

I was a broken woman with little hope for tomorrow,

And only expected heartaches and continual sorrow.

Then one day Jesus met me in my valley of disappointments and pain;

He touched and healed my broken places and made me whole again.

Bring the Savior your broken pieces and hear His loving voice;

I am the Lord who healeth those who make Me their choice.

Don't depend on others or things to make you feel complete,

For they are only substitutes for God and will lead to defeat.

I am a single person, who has grown in God's grace,

To know I am complete because of Christ's embrace.

Chapter Four

What Is Success?

In Chapter One of my book, **One is a Whole Number (Successful Single Living from a Christian's Perspective)**, I defined successful single living. Fourteen years later I am still in agreement with how I defined success. It was definitely a revelation from God. Within this chapter I will present the edited version of the chapter entitled *What Is Success*? Here it is…

When God first began to impress upon me to write a book about successful single living, I was hesitant because I wasn't sure if I were a successful single person. I didn't want to write about something unless I was first experiencing it myself. This is a principle I live by.

If I were a successful single person, I believed I would not struggle at anytime with any aspect of my singleness. There would be no loneliness, frustration, gloomy days, or a desire for companionship. When I arrived at this imaginary place of single bliss, I would always be content, wake up every morning with a song on my lips and a smile on my face. I would be so thrilled about being single; it wouldn't matter if I ever got married.

Cinderella needed to wake up from her fantasy. The above belief was an imaginary state of single blissfulness—idealistic but not realistic. Before I could write a book about successful living, I needed a balanced view which could only come from God. He is a God of order and balance and doesn't set impossible goals for His children. We oftentimes demand more of ourselves than we are capable of achieving. But God knows we are only clay and that without divine intervention we will not reach our full potential.

The idea about writing about successful single living came sometime in the year 1985 when I was twenty-two years old. It came shortly after I had made a comment to a girl I worked with that I wanted to marry a successful man. I heard someone say when a woman chooses a husband she chooses a lifestyle. Therefore, I felt that after all the years of waiting for a husband I should reach for the sky. Anyone less than what I imagined in my mind would not be accepted. A poor man without degrees, house, looks or social status would not even be considered. Miss Gwen wanted everyone to "ooh" and "ah" when she got married. The words I wanted to hear were: "It sure paid off for her to wait as long as she did." (This book was written in phases, so I am not sure at what age I decided I had been waiting a long time.) I wanted God's best and I was convinced that His best was based on outward accomplishments and qualities. Marrying a man with superior outward qualities and accomplishments would glorify God. In reality it was I who wanted the glory. After making the statement that I wanted to marry a successful man, God spoke to me and said, "I want to make you successful." From that day on I set out to learn and understand success from God's point of view.

Many years passed before I understood why God wanted me to be successful. He didn't want me to be dependent on someone else's success because circumstances change. A person can be successful today and filing for bankruptcy tomorrow. Corporate CEOs and presidents resign and are fired as quickly as they are hired. Successful ministries have gone under and great men and women of God have fallen. Women married men who they thought had great wealth, but later found out they had more debt than wealth.

The Psalmist issued a warning: "If riches increase, set not your heart upon them." "It is better to trust in the Lord than to put confidence in man." God is the only One Who will not change. He will always be Jehovah-jireh and El Shaddai—Our Great Provider, the God Who is more than enough.

There was a time in which the word, success, would not have been used to describe single living. To be successful meant you had to be married and have a family. Together you and your mate would work together to acquire the things that symbolized success such as buying a house, the furnishings that go in it, a car and put money aside to take family vacations. The man was usually diligently climbing the corporate ladder or working hard at whatever the profession he had chosen.

If you weren't married by a certain age, people began to wonder if there was something wrong with us. Our single status often became the topic of conversations at many family gatherings. Match-making became some of our relatives' favorite pastime whether we asked for their help or not. Every wedding brought either the unwanted question, "When are you going to get married?", or the worn-out cliché, "You'll be next." Others made jokes about our single status, and we tried to keep smiling. Many times we experienced pain and frustration once again from those who professed to love us so much.

We were made to feel like misfits or rejects in a society that did not offer much hope for the unmarried person. Even our places of worship failed to give us hope or consolation. The worship services and program were geared towards the family unit, especially during holidays. Everything centered on strengthening and bettering family relationships. Singles were made to feel that whatever problems they were facing were really not important, unless they were divorced or a single parent. Real problems occurred only in marriages.

Years have passed and changes have occurred. Society's view of single living has changed. Success is now considered to be a goal for singles to obtain. We can set solo goals and buy houses, cars, climb the corporate ladder and be termed "successful". In fact, because of the turmoil in marriages, singles are sometimes lauded in this generation for their decision to remain single.

Yet for the Christian single, our singleness is still a source of concern. There are innate desires and longings that still must be dealt with. The world cannot offer us any real life solutions. Although our society feels it is all right to be single, many also feel it is acceptable to be immoral, promiscuous, and to live undisciplined lives. They shout, "If it feels good, go ahead and do it." However, the words of King Solomon written in the book of Ecclesiastes issue a warning to every generation, especially to the youth.

"Rejoice, O young man, in your youth, And let your heart cheer you in the day of your youth; Walk in the ways of your heart, And in the sight of your eyes; But know that for all these God will bring you into judgment." (Ecclesiastes 11:9)

God requires us to live pure lives and that is something which will never change. One day we will stand before Him and give an account of the choices we made. Christian singles are not asked to make the right decisions on their own, but you can lean on Jesus who continually says: "Come to Me, all you who labor and are heaven laden, and I will give your rest. Take my yoke upon you and learn from Me, for I am gentle and lowly in heart, and you will find rest for your souls."

You can go to Him when you can't go to anyone else. He understands and He cares about the struggles the single face. For He lived as a single person while on earth and is acquainted with the challenges we face.

Singles must resolve their issues now and stop believing that marriage will solve all. If two single people bring all their unresolved problems into a marriage, that marriage is destined to become a great battlefield that may not endure the emotional explosions. Success must be discovered now while you are single.

So what is success? There are different opinions as to what it means to be successful. Some believe success is climbing the corporate ladder and acquiring a lot of tangible things. They are willing to spend countless hours striving for success at the expense of losing touch with their families and damaging their health both physically and emotionally.

Unfortunately, sometimes after they have acquired all the things that symbolize success they feel empty rather than fulfilled. You can hear them say, "Is this all there is?" It is not uncommon to read about a person who reached the peak of his or her career, was socially well known, accepted and respected, but then the roof seemly caved in. They were unable to cope with life. They became alcoholics, addicted to drugs, or even worse—they committed suicide. What causes people to give up when it seems they have so much going for them, so much to live for? No doubt it is because they didn't have a solid, current relationship with God. God alone is the only true success factor, Who has stood the test of time.

Anything or person not founded upon Him will eventually fail. He makes living worthwhile, and regardless of what we acquired in life, it is our relationship with Him that counts the most. In Jeremiah 9:23, 24 God said:

"Let not the wise man glory in his wisdom, Let not the mighty man glory in his might, Nor let the rich man glory in his riches; But let him who glories glory in this, That he understands and knows Me, that I am the Lord, exercising lovingkindness, judgment, and righteous in the earth. For in these I delight, says the Lord."

God created us for His purpose and pleasure. Unless you fulfill His plan of having a love relationship with Him, you will never arrive at real success. This relationship can only be created by accepting Jesus into your life as your personal Lord and Savior. Revelations 4:11 reveals,

"Thou are worthy, O Lord, to receive glory and honor and power: for thou has created all things, and for thy pleasure they are and were created."

When we fail to admit to the fact that we were created for God's pleasure and continually go away from Him, we will experience loneliness and emptiness. There is not anything in this world that can take God's place. The atheist claims to be happy without God, but the Psalmist wrote in Psalms 14:1:

"The fool has said in his heart, There is no God. They are corrupt, They have done abominable works, There is none who does good."

When you deny the existence of God, you deny the only real foundation for happiness in this world. If they would be honest with themselves, they would admit that there is a deep longing within for something greater than themselves.

Let's answer the question, what is success, more thoroughly. Success is:

➢ **Obeying the will of God—Living a life pleasing to Him**. Jesus said in Luke 11:28, "More than that, blessed are those who hear the word of God and keep it!" Everything else hinges on obedience to the Word of God.

➢ **Being content.** In I Timothy we read: "But godliness with contentment is great gain." (NIV)

Further, if there are any places in your life where you suffer lack, you can trust God to provide for you. We have the assurance in Philippians 4:19:

"And my God shall supply all your need according to His riches in glory by Christ Jesus."

If you can't find happiness where you are, you won't find it anywhere else. We all need to come to the place where we can say like Paul in Philippians 4: 11:

"Not that I speak in regard to need, for I have learned in whatever state I am, to be content.

Knowing that you are responsible for your success. It is a choice that only you can make.

Reaping or receiving the benefits of blessings of living a life in obedience to God. That might mean promotions, good health, a supportive family and friends, material wealth, or a successful ministry. Yet don't get hung up on the externals as signs of true success. For one time when I was upset over not making the amount of money I thought I deserved God said, "Gwen, you can't measure my blessings in dollars and cents."

We too often overlook the most important things in life that money can't buy such as peace, joy, love, contentment, good health, good friends, a loving family, but most importantly a loving relationship with God who is our greatest Asset. Obeying God is the only way you will discover the best plan to live your life.

God has a plan for all of our lives and if we submit to that plan, we will achieve the maximum in our lives. We read in Jeremiah 29:11

"For I know the plans I have for you, declares the Lord, plans to prosper you and not harm you, plans to give you hope and a future."

This plan of success is not dependent upon whether we are married or single, but it has to do with our relationship with God. Many singles have put off trying to achieve success in hopes of finding Mr. or Miss Right, believing that that person will help them to obtain success. The truth we must all learn is this: Unless we can learn to be successful on our own, we may not find it with anyone else.

Success is first inward (responding in loving obedience to God) and then it flows outward. It's an individual thing. Through obedience to God's Word we will find strength to be all we were meant to be and courage to possess those tangible and intangible things that are ours.

Learning how to be successful is a task within itself. There are struggles, disappointments, frustrated plans and dreams that will never come to pass. There are failures and mistakes we encounter. No one can know true success without having experienced failure first. Yet we must be determined that we will not allow mistakes and failures to stop us from reaching our place of destiny. Allow them to be our building blocks for building stronger character.

God is our creator and the Divine Potter, and we are the clay in His hands. As the Psalmist declared in Psalms 138:8, "The Lord will perfect that which concerns me;"

Also, Paul wrote in Philippians 1:6, "Being confident of this very thing, that He who has begun a good work in you will complete it until the day of Jesus Christ;"

Although others may give up on us, God never will. Failure is inevitable, but I heard someone say that "success is getting up one more time than you're knocked down." Success knows that there is a God greater than all the mistakes we will make in our lives, and that we can claim Romans 8:28 as our own personal inspiration.

"And we know that all things work together for good to those who love God, those who are the called according to His purpose."

Many of the things we go through don't seem or feel good, but God's divine purpose is to bring the good out of the most painful situations we go through. We are called to be overcomers, knowing that we are more than conquerors through Christ. We must be determined that neither life nor death, nor things present, nor things to come, not even the difficulties of our singleness will separate us from the love of God. His love will transform our lives continually to make us what we are destined to be.

In our quest for success, singles will have to learn to cope with difficult situations such as: our need for love, loneliness, rejection, heartaches, disappointments, depression, need for wholeness, sexual temptations, etc. We must know before we encounter them that they can't defeat us unless we allow them to.

Marriage is not a solution for all problems. If you marry the wrong person, those problems will escalate.

The method for overcoming these difficulties, which has stood the test of time, is following the instructions from the Word of God. Do what God has commanded us to do. The word of God is the only lasting foundation upon which to build our lives.

Jesus told the parable in the 7th Chapter of Matthew about two builders who chose different materials upon which to build the foundation of their homes, which is symbolic of our lives.

The parable begins as such:

"Therefore, whoever hears these sayings of Mine, and does them, I will liken him to a wise man who built his house on the rock: and the rain descended, the floods came, and the winds blew and beat on that house; and it did not fall, for it was founded on the rock.

But everyone who hears these sayings of Mine, and does not do them, will be like a foolish man who built his house on the sand: and the rain descended the floods came, and the winds blew and beat on that house; and it fell. And great was its fall."

Both men were faced with a vehement storm of wind and rain, which are representative of all the adverse things that come into our lives. Yet the results were different. The results were according to each man's response to the words Jesus spoke.

For the person who obeyed Jesus, he was able to go through victoriously. When we do what Jesus said, He will either calm the storm or give you the grace to go through. Success is not avoiding storms, but it is successfully going through them. For the person who ignored Jesus' words, he suffered ultimate failure.

In Chapter Five we will discuss some of the perplexities that plague the singles more in depth. We will discover over and over again how drawing the truths from the Word of God will enable us to overcome obstacles. Obeying these truths will cause us to live continuously as a successful single person.

This book does not claim to be the answer or solution for every single's problem. Yet if it helps to alleviate some of the pressures of being single, it will have served its purpose. Singles rise above defeat and discouragement, and begin to live victoriously as a successful single person.

Chapter Five

Fourteen Years Later—The Struggles are the Same

Here we are fourteen years later. Have things really changed that much for the Christian single? Are the struggles really the same? I believe they are. How do you define the word struggle? The answer can be defined by the following words: battle, fight, disagreement, clash, encounter, scuffle, conflict, and confrontation. You get the picture. The reason the single's issues are described as struggles is because we are required to resolve them in a Godly fashion. That goes completely against the grain of our nature. Society is constantly teaching and screaming at us that it is not necessary to handle these issues God's way. People in the church tell us through their actions it is not necessary to handle them the Godly way. No wonder so many singles are still confused and rush into marriage hoping to put these issues to rest. They want to quiet the noises in their heads and hearts.

Marriage alone was never meant to resolve all these issues. Disappointment is what many couples experience within the marital relationship. Why? We'll discuss this more in detail issue by issue. The subsections are as follows:

♥   A Quest for Love

♥   Living Through Loneliness

♥   Coping with Sexuality

♥   Recovering from Rejection

♥   What Do You Do When Your Heart Has Been Broken?

A Quest for Love

In my first book I wrote that love was the greatest need that singles had in their lives. Fourteen years later I still believe that to be true. They may not express their need in those exact words, but the sentiment will be the same. You may have to read between the lines. Oftentimes we hear even strong and independent people making the following statements:

- ➢ I wish I could find someone who would want me for myself apart from anything I have or do.

- ➢ Someone who would care enough to sit and listen to how I really feel without judging me

- ➢ Someone who would accept me just as I am without criticizing or constantly trying to change me

- ➢ Someone who would understand my varying moods

- ➢ Someone who would overlook my faults and appreciate my strengths

- ➢ Someone who would be a real friend and offer me encouragement and comfort when I need it the most

They are simply saying I want someone to love me. Most of us expect human love to do what only the love of God is designed to do. Our human spirits are constantly crying out to be loved by God, to experience deep intimacy with Him, to be satiated and satisfied in the deepest recesses of our souls. That longing can only be satisfied as we spend time in the presence of God in prayer, praise and worship.

Because we are not aware that God has put a longing within our spirits for Him, we mistakenly believe that Mr. or Miss Right can fill that void in our lives that is meant for God only. When human love fails to meet our unrealistic expectations, we often find ourselves with a broken heart and we are very unhappy.

For years I went in search of a love that could satisfy me like only the love of God is designed to do. The following poem was written in November of 1986. It was a major breakthrough in my life. I finally realized that the type of love I needed could only be found in God. As you read this poem, you will discover I had high expectations and disappointments. Yet I later experienced the satisfying love of God which changed my life.

A SEARCH FOR LOVE

By Gwendolyn J. Wheeler

For so many years I dreamed of someone who would impart,

A romantic love to me which would satisfy my longing heart.

I searched and I searched, and I prayed and I prayed,

For that certain man to come and take my loneliness away.

Someone who would share the good times as well as the bad,

And whose mere presence could keep me from feeling sad.

Someone who would be sensitive and tell from my face,

When I needed encouragement or just a gentle embrace.

Someone to dream my dreams and see what I see,

As clearly as I could see, as though he were me.

Someone who would be content if we went for a walk,

Or just sat alongside the beach engaged in small talk.

But one day God spoke words I really needed to hear,

Words that were soothing with a message so clear.

Gwen Wheeler, I am what you are looking for;

Stop searching my child, and don't look anymore.

Not a man on earth can meet the expectations you have set;

Yet through Me all those needs have already been met.

I have always loved you greatly with an everlasting love,

And have the kind of love you need which is from above.

So if you are searching for love, don't look any further,

For God is real love and He satisfies like none other.

God may still give you a companion to really love you,

But while you are waiting you don't have to be blue.

You must live each day fully, doing all that you can,

Telling of God's gift of life through the Son of Man.

Jesus has been a friend through good and stormy weather,

And all of life's adversities have brought us closer together.

He loves me dearly and taught me what love is all about;

He makes me so joyful that I just want to run and shout:

He loves me! He loves me! And that love has set me free,

To grow and become the woman God has called me to be.

My search for love is over, and I'm happy to say,

I'm experiencing magnificent and real love every day.

♥♥♥♥♥♥♥♥♥♥♥♥♥♥♥♥♥♥♥♥♥♥♥♥♥♥♥♥♥♥♥♥♥♥♥♥♥♥♥

My discovery of the purest love, God's love, set me free from my own prison of unrealistic expectations. God's freedom conditioned my heart to know and appreciate true human love when it came into my life. I no longer expect human love to be what only God's love can be.

Many singles need to be freed from their prison of false expectations. This prison no doubt has been built over a long period of time. Jesus said, "You shall know the truth, and the truth shall make you free."

The truth so many must accept is that they don't know what real love is. Romance has been mistaken for love. We associate love with candlelight dinners, roses sent unexpectedly, moonlight walks along the beach, love notes sent on perfumed stationery, and stars in our eyes and music in our heart. If some of these things are absent, we don't consider it real love.

Many good relationships were aborted because the other person failed to live up to our romantic expectations. People's backgrounds are different and everyone does not express love in the same way. Singles must allow others to express love in the way that is comfortable to them. Who is to say that the way you think love should be expressed is the correct way?

Love could have passed you by without you knowing it. The sadder part is that many couples got married on an emotional/romantic high. Before they could even discover what real love is they found themselves in the divorce courts. They were frustrated and angry over the fact that the other person refused to live out their fantasy of love.

Love's true meaning and source is found in the Word of God. Galatians 5:22 allows us to see that love is a fruit of the Spirit. It is a fruit that is birthed and developed in the human spirit by the Holy Spirit.

Love is a gift of God. James 1:17 says: "Every good gift and every perfect gift is from above, and comes down from the Father of lights, with whom there is no variation or shadow of turning."

The definition of love is endless. A few facts that describe true love are as follows:

- ➢ Love is a commitment to take an active part in another person's life.

- ➢ It is a decision to care about someone and to share part of you even when that sharing requires painful interaction.

- ➢ Love does not mean you will meet all their needs. None of us are equipped to do that.

- ➢ It does mean to the best of your ability you will reach out and touch their life with your talents and qualities.

- ➢ Love is giving and forgiving, forbearing, and tolerating faults in others.

- ➤ It is showing kindness, understanding, trust and respect.

- ➤ It means risking to communicate—telling the other person how you feel. Being open to listen to their point of view even if it is different from yours.

- ➤ Love is sharing the good times as well as the bad, which involves praying for them, as well as comforting and encouraging them.

- ➤ It is giving a person the benefit of the doubt even though circumstances may dictate that you do otherwise.

- ➤ But it doesn't mean that you put yourself in harm's way and allow another person to misuse or abuse you.

- ➤ Love is giving a person all the freedom and space they need to grow and develop into the unique person God has called them to be.

There are many peaks and valleys in relationships. Being in love is not always a pleasant experience. There are hurts, frustrations, and many disappointments. There are interruptions and delays. Some stuff you deal with sometimes doesn't make any sense. At other times there is so much happiness and laughter. Good times and special moments cause us to fall in love all over again. Wonderful surprises appear just when we need them the most. Love can be warm and cozy one moment and a chilling winter wind on another day. Paul gave us some interesting characteristics of love. He wrote, "Love suffers long and is kind; bears all things, believes all things, hopes all things, endures all things."

As we grow older, some of those things we thought were important are no longer an issue. Love and life mature us, and we learn that agreeing on peace is more important than trying to agree on every issue. Loving each other requires that we compromise and forgive each other continuously.

The definition of love needs to be reevaluated by some singles. This waiting period is a gift from God. He has spared you from the disappointment and pain that an unrealistic view of love can bring.

Before you enter into a growing and healthy relationship, you need to understand the true meaning of love. Allow the Holy Spirit to sift all the imaginary ideas out of you and pour all the real definitions into you. As your definition of love matures, it will demand you to grow as well.

It is important that you understand we are all human with faults and weaknesses. Everyone gets tired, frustrated, irritated, irritable, and have mood changes (more often than not). Some days we are difficult to get along with. We can be insensitive, unreasonable, stubborn, unlovable, unforgiving, and preoccupied with other things. It takes more than human love to put up with us at times.

God is the only person who is capable of loving us totally without any reservations. He loved us when we are at our worst. Before we were formed in our mother's womb, He loved us and proved that love. Romans 5:8 declares "But God demonstrates His own love toward us, in that while we were still sinners, Christ died for us." John wrote: "This is love, not that we loved God, but that He loved us and sent His Son as an atoning sacrifice for our sins."

We need to sit down at the foot of Calvary and take some lessons from Christ regarding what it really means to love. Our view of real love will change, and we will discover that it is more important to give love than to receive it. This transition will cause us to pray differently about that special person we will marry whether we have met him or her. We will ask God to teach us how to love them. This prayer will allow the Holy Spirit to plant the fruit of love within our spirits. When we come together with our mates, we won't waste precious time arguing over things that do not have anything to do with love. Our love will be pure, unselfish, and very powerful. It will not only transform both of our lives, but the lives of those we come in contact with. Just think what a powerful witness that will be to those who don't know Jesus.

Always remember that God is the author of love and only He can teach us how to love Him, love others, and love ourselves. Part of becoming a whole person involves learning to love our self. I am grateful that God taught me how to love, like, accept and appreciate who I am. Christian self-love is not narcissism—excessive love or admiration of oneself. Instead it is a Godly, healthy love that promotes positive self-worth.

As a young girl I didn't like myself and craved for the approval of another; I was shy and withdrawn. My self-esteem was very low and prevented me from being able to look anyone in the face for too long. I would immediately look back at the ground or floor. That passage of my life was called the "the ugly duckling" period.

If you met me now and heard me speak in private or public, you would find it difficult to believe I ever struggled with shyness or self-worth. My cure for this lack of self-worth and shyness is the love of God. I came to know Him at the age of 14 and He transformed my life. He showed me the beauty within and without, told me I was special, and cared for me so personally and tenderly. His love made the difference in my life and kept me from becoming a desperate or needy person.

My father died from cancer when I was 15 years old, and without the divine intervention of God my life would have gone in a wrong direction. When I was young, I was very impressionable and easy to be led astray. I could have become an unwed mother, drug addict or even an alcoholic. Negative factors could have caused me to lose my way so easily. I am grateful that a more powerful factor was present—the God factor. For that reason I cannot pat myself on the back or congratulate myself for having escaped the perils that lie within society. To God be the glory for all that He has done!

God has protected, shielded, and delivered me from wrong relationships and situations. He has forgiven and restored me from mistakes that I made. I have not lived this single life perfectly, but He still loves me anyway. Being whole does not mean we are perfect, but it means we are forgiven and restored. I owe Him my life and there are no words I can say to adequately express my gratitude.

Growing up as a child we didn't have many material things; we were definitely poor. When my father died, he had no material inheritance to leave us. Yet he left us a legacy of Godly principles to live by and an example of what true love is. He loved his family. The greatest and most profound thing he did for his children was to love our mother. I am grateful for that. He died forty years ago, and my mother's face still lights up when she talks about him. They were married almost twenty-six years. By the way, my dad was a very romantic person. He would give my mother more than one card, because he said one card could not tell her how much he loved her. He bought flowers and candy for her. In my mind that was how love was supposed to be demonstrated.

Some of you reading this book did not have such a Godly example of love. God will make up for the fathering you didn't get. Open up to Him and allow Him to love you. Allow His love to heal you. Without His healing you will always be emotionally crippled. You'll never be able to fully love God, yourself or anyone else. The greatest need you have is to be loved by God, especially when you are hurting and broken. Don't make the mistake of using a human relationship to be a Band-aid to cover your pain. People will fail you and that hidden pain will rupture and more pain will occur. I talk about that in the subsection on Recovering from Rejection.

Remember the words of my poem: "God may give you a companion to really love you, but while you are waiting you don't have to be blue." On the other hand, if God doesn't give you a companion to love you, you still don't have to be blue. God's love is better than any human love could ever be. Just open up and allow Him to love you into being a whole person.

Living Through Loneliness

How can loneliness be defined? To some it means the absence of human companionship. It can be defined as the intense longing to have someone share one's life. It is an aching emptiness in your heart that reminds you that you have not united with someone who shares mutual interests, concerns, and goals.

Marriage is not necessarily a remedy for loneliness. During a church outing a group of single women were complaining about how lonely they were. To our surprise, a couple of married women said, "We are lonely, too!" There are married people who do not share common goals or interests. They live in the same house, have physical contact occasionally, but their hearts and interests are valleys apart. They are in fact lonely.

What an unfortunate situation to find oneself in. People married mates believing that loneliness would be a thing of the past. How painful it must be to discover that loneliness is still something they experience too frequently.

When I wrote about love, I said, "Love does not mean you will meet all their needs. None of us are equipped to do that." Therefore, even the best marriages can experience loneliness at times. Yet there are those who experience loneliness on a regular basis. Silent tears are the only company they know.

Clearly, it is wise counsel to singles to find creative and healthy ways to deal with loneliness. You may have to use that same creativity within your marriage. Let me stop here and state one fact. Being single doesn't mean that you are going to be lonely all the time.

Years ago when I first began to rewrite this section, I had a difficult time at first. I had grown and changed so much. The life I lived then and now is a very full one; loneliness is not an everyday occurrence. Therefore, trying to define loneliness took some soul searching and reaching back in order to remember how it felt. Exhaustion sometimes seems to be more of a companion than loneliness is.

Being a pastor, a writer, an entrepreneur developing my first for profit business, Sensational Floral Designs By Gwendolyn, being a family member, exercising, grocery shopping, and just dealing with the responsibilities of home ownership are juggling acts. There are days I am so tired and emotionally drained. When I get home, I am grateful that a husband and children are not there waiting for my attention. Rest and solitude are the companions I desire. As a single woman, I have a lot of freedom that would be limited if I were married.

Yet even this busy, independent, strong Black woman is not exempt from loneliness. Most of the time when it appears it is a brief encounter. Then there are the days when loneliness is like a bad cold—it lingers a lot longer than anticipated. Those experiences help me to stay balanced. If I am going to minister to others, then I need to be able to relate to what they feel.

For the single person, the reality of loneliness can strike at anytime and anywhere. It can happen while you are by yourself or when you are in a crowd. The normal affairs of life where couples are more visible such as worship services, family gatherings, and high school reunions create an atmosphere for loneliness. More difficult are holidays and special occasions such as Christmas, Thanksgiving, Valentine's Day, weddings, and your birthday. These are affairs made for sharing.

When loneliness hits, we need to find creative ways of dealing with or alleviating it. It is important to refocus your attention on something else other than yourself. Life gives you choices. How are you going to deal with your loneliness? Will you choose to go home, sit in a corner, be depressed and have a pity party? That choice will not accomplish anything. In fact, being depressed and feeling sorry for yourself are wasted energies. Depression can drain you and take away the joy of everyday living. It can camouflage your blessings and make you think no one cares about you, not even God. When I speak of depression, I am talking about temporarily feeling sad or unhappy about situations in your life.

If you are suffering from a deeper depression commonly referred to as Clinical Depression, you need to seek professional help. I am not in the medical profession, so I cannot speak on this subject from an expert's point of view. I can share what I read and ask that you do your own research. Clinical depression has been defined as a psychotic disorder marked especially by sadness, inactivity, difficulty with thinking and concentration. People suffering from this experience a significant increase or decrease in their appetite, have trouble sleeping, experience feelings of dejection, hopelessness, and sometimes have suicidal thoughts or attempt to commit suicidal. Get professional help right away. Yes, sometimes people in the church need professional help; they need more than a change of attitude and routine. Unless they allow God to heal them, they need the aid of a professional person that can help them through their depression. God is a healer, but their faith may not have reached that level yet. <u>Let them get help</u>.

For those of you dealing with temporary depression, get up and do something creative. Some suggestions are:

- ➤ Get together with some good, positive friends who will pray for you and have good conversation. A conversation that will cause you to laugh and smile.

- ➤ Can't meet them? Call some positive friends on the phone

- ➤ Take yourself out to a nice restaurant.

- ➤ Go to a spa and be pampered or pamper yourself at home.

- ➤ Live near a beach or water? Go take a long walk or a swim

- ➤ Like to read? Crawl up in a chair with a good book.

- ➤ Own a home and enjoy gardening? Go work in your garden or rearrange some stuff in your home

- Like to drive? Go for a nice long ride.

- Enjoy physical activities? Ride your bike or go to the gym and workout.

- Christian concert at your church? Buy a ticket and go and be uplifted.

- Got cable TV—turn to the Christian stations and be inspired

- Whatever you do, also remember to pray. Ask God for strength, peace, joy and guidance.

- Play some good Christian music and sing along. Let those words get down in your spirit and lift you up. The presence of God will fill your home or car. God can give you a song to sing in the midst of loneliness that will cheer you up. One night years ago I was scheduled to speak at a single's meeting. I had to drive about 40 miles at night (one way) by myself. I began to feel a little down and lonely. God brought these words to my mind: **"Never alone, I don't have to worry because I'm never alone. He walks beside me every day. He guides my footsteps along the way. Never alone, I don't have to worry because I'm never alone."** Those words brought joy and strength to my heart. I was reminded again that although I had no human companion I was not alone. That night I spoke words of hope to the other singles. It is very seldom that I have to go by myself. God usually allows someone else to go with me. He has blessed me with wonderful Christian friends. We have good fellowship.

If you don't have some good Christian friends with whom you can have fellowship, pray and ask God to send some. Proverbs 18:24 gives us further insight about friendship. "A man that hath friends must shew himself friendly: and there is a friend that sticketh closer than a brother." The body of Christ is big enough to provide you with friends. You may not be married right now, but you don't have to be alone. Scriptures say we are helpers one to another. Friends can help to alleviate those feelings of loneliness.

If friends are not available when you need them, remember you can always call on God and He will come to your rescue. Sometimes friends have other plans and you are not a part of those plans. You can admit to God that you are lonely and you need Him to touch you and bring relief. Notice I did not say beg and ask Him for a husband or wife. God works according to seasons; this may not be your season for marriage. Some people take matters into their own hands and later wish they had waited.

Psalmist wrote: "When my heart is overwhelmed within lead me to a Rock that is higher than I." Loneliness can be overwhelming at times, but you can successfully get through it.

Alone hours can be an opportunity to get to know God better. There is so much about Him that we haven't even begun to learn. In knowing God better, we will learn to trust Him more and appreciate even the adverse circumstances that come into our lives such as loneliness. We will discover that there is a gift or blessing wrapped in every painful situation. It takes time and patience to unravel the gift. At 55 I am still unraveling gifts. Don't let that scare you. You may not have to be single as long as I have.

The greatest lesson I have learned is that the greatest friend you will ever have is Jesus Christ. He is my continual listening ear and shoulder to lean on. I am reminded of the words of an old hymn that used to be my father's favorite.

"What a friend we have in Jesus, all our griefs and sins to bear, what a privilege to carry everything to God in prayer. Oh, what peace we often forfeit, Oh what needless pain we bear, all because we do not carry everything to God in prayer."

Another one is similar:

"There's not a friend like the lowly Jesus, No, not one! No not one! None else could heal all my soul's diseases, No, not one, No, not one! Jesus knows all about our struggles. He will guide til the day is done;"

Hebrews 4:15, 16 says it this way:

"For we do not have a High Priest who cannot sympathize with our weaknesses, but was in all points tempted as we are, yet without sin. Let us therefore come boldly to the throne of grace, that we may obtain mercy and find grace to help in time of need."

If anyone knows about loneliness Jesus does. It was mighty lonely upon that cross the day He died and cried out, "My God, My God, why has thou forsaken me." Some of you who are single feel lonely and forsaken by God, but He hasn't forsaken you. He said, "I will never leave or forsake you." There was a purpose for Jesus' aloneness and there is a purpose for yours. God knows something that you don't know; you must trust His wisdom even if He doesn't reveal it to you.

Alone times don't have to be lonely times. They can be times that you discover talents, skills, and gifts that lie dormant within you. There may be a business you are to start, a ministry waiting to be birthed, a country to visit, or even a book waiting to be written. A song or a play may be about to emerge that the world will never see or hear unless you write them. Another part of your destiny is waiting to be embraced by you. Your singleness is not an accident, my friend. Find out what you are called to do today. You are wonderfully and uniquely made.

May you discover in a fresh new way how God, El Shaddai, is more than enough! Get up out of the pit of loneliness and begin to enjoy the God given pleasures. Look around and discover the joys of living. You are not alone in your struggle.

Coping with Sexuality

With all the confusion about sexual relationships today, one might think that God made a mistake when he created such an alluring passion within the human make-up. Yet sexuality is not a mistake. After God had finished creating everything, Genesis 1:12 declares, "Then God saw everything that He had made, and indeed it was very good. So the evening and the morning were the sixth day." So what happened to what God pronounced was very good? The writer of Ecclesiastes wrote: "Lo, this only have I found, that God hath made man upright; but they have sought out many inventions (or devices for evil)."

When God created man and woman, He made us on purpose to be sexual beings. He created us to be attracted to the person of the opposite sex. I believe it was God's original plan for everyone to enjoy companionship, intimacy and sexual fulfillment within marriage. This fulfillment was to be part of the benefit of living in Paradise (Garden of Eden). Yet we know the tragic account of man's disobedience which resulted in his fall. Sin separated man from God and caused him to be driven out of Paradise.

Since we no longer live in Paradise, but are living in a world marred by sin, there are some facts we must be aware of:

1.　　Everyone will <u>not</u> get married and singleness will exist until the end of the world.

2.　　Sex is a gift from God to be enjoyed between a man and a woman within the sanctity of marriage.

That has not and will not change—marriage is a union between a man and a woman. Don't write me because the Word of God does not change to fit society's promiscuities or confusion. In Genesis 2 we read:

21) And the Lord God caused a deep sleep to fall upon Adam; and while he slept, He took one of his ribs or a part of his side and closed up the [place with] flesh.

22) And the rib or part of his side which the Lord God had taken from the man He built up and made into a woman, and He brought her to the man.

23) Then Adam said, This [creature] is now bone of my bones and flesh of my flesh; she shall be called Woman, because she was taken out of a man.

24) Therefore a man shall leave his father and his mother and shall become united and cleave to his wife, and they shall become one flesh."

3.　　Christian singles are expected to keep their passions under control and not commit fornication, which is sexual intercourse between two single people—male and female.

4.　　God gives us the ability to control those passions if we follow the guidelines He has set through His Word.

We must obey the voice of the Holy Spirit Who commands us not to give into our sinful cravings. The Scripture that adequately describes the battle that exists between the flesh and the Spirit is Galatians 5:16:17:

16) "This I say then, Walk in the Spirit, and ye shall not fulfil the lust of the flesh.

17) For the flesh lusteth against the Spirit, and the Spirit against the flesh: and these are contrary the one to the other: so that ye cannot do the things that ye would."

The word, walk, in the above Scriptures speaks of our free will, our choice to either obey the promptings of the Spirit or the desires of the flesh. If you obey the Spirit's voice, then you are walking in the Spirit and you will not fulfill or satisfy your fleshly longings or fall into immorality.

Paul wrote these words in I Corinthians 7:19:

"But if they have not self-control (restraint of their passions), they should marry. For it is better to marry than to be aflame (with passion and tortured continually with ungratified desire)." (Amplified Bible)

Some of you may have read the above Scripture and said that's nice, Paul, but you can't get married by yourself. Furthermore, having sex should not be your main reason for getting married. What do you do in the meantime?

Throughout time Satan has glorified sex to the singles. He has deceived them into believing it is the ultimate satisfaction and thrill that they have been missing out on. Our archenemy has no new tricks, because the old ones still work. What worked on Eve works on folks today. He makes them feel that God is being unjust in forbidding them to indulge in acts that temporarily satisfy their flesh. The truth of the matter is this—sin never satisfies. You lose rather than gain. The singles who indulge in premarital sex hurts themselves. The Bible says they sin against themselves. (I Corinthians 6:18)

Paul wrote in I Corinthians 6:13:

"Now the body is not for sexual immorality but for the Lord, and the Lord for the body."

We must all bring our bodies under control of the Holy Spirit, and do not let our bodies control us. We are governed by a higher power than the power of the flesh which urges us to sin. That higher power is the law of God which says:

"For you were bought at a price; therefore glorify God in your body and your spirit, which are God's." (I Corinthians 6:20)

And how do we glorify God? By not yielding to sexual temptation which is sin. Sexual temptation is something that we will all face. Satan will make sure of that. Yet through Christ we all have the power to overcome.

Many Christians are still confused about the issue of abstinence before marriage. Yet Scripture is clear about the subject. The Scriptures I have given are not written in a parable nor are they mysteries that need to be unlocked.

God commands us as singles not to commit fornication. This is not a debatable issue. The world keeps changing it rules, but God's word about this subject is forever settled in heaven—if you are single—don't indulge.

After I wrote my first book, a young lady walked up to me and said, "I don't fit into what you wrote in your book." In other words, because she had children out of wedlock she felt she was not successful. Others will join in with her and say yes we have fallen, too. Since we have been saved, we made mistakes in this area of sexual temptation and have fallen. So I guess that makes us failures. No, falling and making mistakes do not make you a failure.

There is forgiveness and restoration. One of the songs that became popular in our generation is by Donnie

McClurkin. He sings, "We fall down but we get up. A saint is just a sinner that fell down but they got up." Someone once wrote, "Success is just getting up one more time than you have been knocked down." Yes, given into sexual sin can be termed as being "knocked down". Some folks didn't plan it or see it coming. If you have fallen down, my friend, you can get up. I John 1:9 declares, "If we confess our sins, he is faithful and just to forgive us our sins, and to cleanse us from all unrighteousness."

Sexual sins are no worse than the other sins that are committed in the church such as pride, greed, lying, stealing, jealousy, envy, indifference, laziness, not doing what God told you to do, not paying your tithes, backbiting, lack of love, showing no mercy, etc. All sins must be confessed and repented of if you expect to be successful in God—married or single. An unwed mother is no more of a disgrace than the person who is sowing discord in the church. We just like to categorize sin in the church—we have the ones that we feel are more acceptable than others. No, sin is sin and must be repented of.

Don't let the devil convince you that you have made too many mistakes and success is now out of your grip. My advice to you is to humble yourself and repent and allow God to reveal His plan to you. You will be surprised to find out that God's plan for your life is still in motion. He has been waiting patiently for you to come back to Him. Success is still in your future. He will allow you to learn from your mistakes and falls and still use you anyway. Somebody is waiting to hear how God turned your failures into kingdom successes. We don't set out to fall or make mistakes, but as I tell my church over and over again—if you fall, get back up!

On the other hand, we need to teach our young people and older singles that it is an honor and privilege to be a virgin until marriage. The media and talk show hosts may try to criticize them, but we as the Body of Christ need to lift our voices as trumpets and declare that chastity before marriage is honored by God. Tell them they don't have to fall.

Christian singles I want to emphasize God wants us to live pure, Godly lives. You don't have to become a victim of immorality, but you can in fact live victorious in this area of your life. A pure life just doesn't happen by chance. You must take steps toward purity by making the right choices. I Corinthians 10:13 declares:

"No temptation has overtaken you except such as is common to man; God is faithful, who will not allow you to be tempted beyond what you are able, but with the temptation will also make the way of escape that you may be able to bear it."

He will make a way of escape but you must obey His voice and commit yourself to purity. You can cope with your sexuality as a single person by submitting it daily to the Lordship of Christ, and following the guidelines He has provided in His Word and prayer. Remember the words written in Philippians 4:3 "I can do all things through Christ which strengtheneth me."

You can be successful even in this area of your struggle, but remember if you by chance have fallen in this area—get back up—you can still be successful through repentance, restoration and forgiveness.

Recovering from Rejection

I want to begin this section with a special message to all the men who rejected me and married someone else. THANK YOU VERY MUCH! Your rejection helped to release me into the plan that God has for my life. At 55 I have such a greater appreciation of the freedom my singleness has afforded me. I have had the freedom to discover, cultivate, and execute the many possibilities inside of me. If you hadn't rejected me, we might have married, and I would never have discovered how complete of a woman I could be by myself. Our marriage would have limited my life and destiny. I probably wouldn't be writing this book, pastoring my own church, be the CEO of my other non-profit organizations, or an entrepreneur with my own business, Sensational Floral Designs By Gwendolyn. No doubt I wouldn't possess this strong degree of feminine confidence.

Let's go on now to the mission of defining and evaluating rejection. The word, reject from which we derive the word rejection means to refuse to accept, recognize, make use of or give affection. Rejection is something that we all face at one time in our lives.

Although there are different occasions which could result in rejection, the rejection that singles like the least is to be rejected by someone of the opposite sex. That rejection is the most humiliating and painful of them all. It could be quite devastating unless a person is very confident.

We all fall short in our ability to see a person's real worth. Rejection usually occurs because people have accumulated data for many years regarding Mr. or Miss Right. That data is not always realistic, because it is usually based on superficial criterion. Rejection based on that criterion sounds like this: a person is not tall enough, pretty or handsome enough, don't have enough education, don't wear nice clothes, their teeth are not straight, we don't like their sense of humor— don't laugh at our corny jokes, and they and their family do not make enough money and are not prestigious enough. The list goes on.

So many high quality people are overlooked because their outward appearances don't measure up to people's superficial ideas. The things that are important are overlooked, and we settle for things that will not add anything of value to building and sustaining a successful relationship.

Rejection can be a gift. That relationship that you wanted so badly could have been a prison of impossible demands. Misery would have been the prize you would have gained. People's personal tastes are a major factor in rejection, and none of us should take rejection personally.

How easy it is for people to accept the fact that people have different tastes when it comes to inanimate objects such as cars and houses. If a house or car is rejected by a person, their rejection does not make that house or car any less valuable in the marketplace. We must accept that same principle to be true for relationships. When you are rejected, you are no less valuable in the marketplace of life. In fact, you are of immeasurable value because when God created you, He said you were very good!

In order to have a positive view of ourselves, we must draw our self worth from God, and know we can say like the Psalmist in Psalms 139:14-16.

"I will praise You, for I am fearfully and wonderfully made; Marvelous are Your works, And that my soul knows very well. My frame was not hidden from You, When I was made in secret, And skillfully wrought in the lowest parts of the earth. Your eyes saw my substance, being yet unformed. And in Your book they all were written, The days fashioned for me, When as yet there were none of them."

Rejection can come in various ways and at various times. It can come at an initial encounter. You find yourself interested in someone, but they don't share the same interest—Rejection occurs.

On another occasion, you may have spent time with someone in a friendship hoping that it would grow into something more only to discover that he or she doesn't want you for anything more than a friend—Rejection occurs.

Worse still is to be within a relationship that was mutually expected to grow into a life-time relationship, but then the other person decided you are not the one. They may have even ended the relationship rather abruptly—Rejection occurs. It is painful to be rejected by someone you spent a considerable amount of time with. You loved them dearly and shared good and bad times together through various seasons, laughing and sometimes crying. To have that person lose interest can be devastating.

That person who rejected you became so much a part of your life and your dreams. You are wondering now how will you survive, and may even feel you don't have a reason to live. Hear me say these words loud and clear—your life is not over! You have a lot of living within you. This dark and painful season will pass and you will get better with the help and strength of the Lord. He is right there with you. Time will pass and this pain one day will only be a distant memory.

Scripture encourages us that "Weeping may endure for a night but joy cometh in the morning." Your morning is coming. Morning is symbolic of a new beginning. God will turn your mourning into dancing and cause you to laugh and smile again. The tears will not last forever and your feeling of hopelessness will disappear. Just hang in there, my friend. God will bring you through this bleak time in your life. God will reward you with peace and joy—two elements necessary for successful living.

I experienced rejection at a young age and developed a fear of rejection. The fear of rejection was so great that it caused me to create an invisible, protective wall to guard my heart from pain. Unfortunately, that protective wall also became a barrier that kept me from developing meaningful relationships. If I thought a man had any intentions of breaking off our relationship, I would break up with him first just to avoid being rejected. For a while I practiced hiding my feelings and not letting the other person know how much I cared. To further guard my heart, I thought I could monitor my emotions and not allow myself to care too much for anyone. I wanted to be able to withdraw my emotions whenever I wanted to. Thus, no one would have the opportunity to take advantage of me and hurt me.

Yet life is not that neatly packaged. You can't monitor your emotions that closely. Sooner or later you will be attracted to someone who is not attracted to you and find yourself being rejected. But as the old cliché goes—this too will pass.

When I was in my mid-twenties I was rejected by someone I thought cared about me. His rejection caused me to desire to die or at least find a large hole that I could crawl into. In Chapter 7 of my book, On the Road to Recovery Again..., I described this person as "A Player in the House of God". Buy my book and read about the greater details of this incident.

In short, this person not only rejected me, but humiliated me as well—a deadly combination. I found myself slipping into what seemed like a daze. Even though I was still conscious of what was happening around me, I was staring into space without even thinking about anything.

If God had not intervened, I would have had a mental breakdown or gone into a deep depression. His mercy and grace jolted me back to my senses, and allowed a friend to say the right thing at the right time. The words she spoke that day allowed me to know God knew this tremendous heartbreak was coming, but His grace would be sufficient enough to take me through it.

This emotional trauma occurred because I became interested in someone else before my heart had adequately healed from a previous relationship. What was meant to be a friendship to help me through my painful ordeal turned into a hurtful disappointment and rejection. He took advantage of a vulnerable situation, and then pretended as though I misunderstood his actions. I never heard the words, I am sorry, from him.

A great lesson was learned from this incident. First, when you feel hurt or rejected, don't use any relationship other than God as a balm, Band-Aid or medicinal solution. That relationship could go sour and what once served as soothing relief can become like acid that will leave you worse than you were in the beginning.

Secondly, you have only one Savior, Healer and Deliverer Who is perfect in every way. His name is Jesus, the righteous Son of God. He died to set you free from sin and bring you into a harmonious relationship with God, the Father. He alone has the right words for you in whatever season you are in. His love and friendship will never turn sour. He will never reject you. God is available anytime that we need Him. He is always on duty 24 hours a day.

Psalms 34:18 tells us "The Lord is near to those who have a broken heart, And saves such as have a contrite spirit."

God has many creative ways to heal you from the sting of rejection. Once while I was visiting my aunt, I experienced rejection. I found it out at the outset of my visit. When I reached the room where I was to stay, there was a vase of flowers with a card. On the envelope were written these words:

"Gwen, the Lord loves you a lot and we do too. I hope you will leave in a new light."

The card inside read:

"The Lord wants you to take this time and rest in Him. He is going to show you a new way. He says, Draw away unto Me and hide yourself in me. Let me take those hidden hurts. Look not to man but unto me for peace and understanding. For my way is strange unto man, but leads to a higher place. I say rest in Me. Lean not on your understanding but unto me." Aunt Eloise

I was scheduled to speak that Saturday at a Prayer Breakfast my aunt had planned. My message that morning was about the peace of God. New insight had come indeed. I continue to learn how to rest in God continuously. There are various degrees of resting in Him, and I am determined to keep climbing until I reach the highest level of rest in Him.

I left Maine in a new light. Although I know my aunt ordered those flowers, it was ordained by God. I still have that green vase today—it reminds me of the day that God cared enough to send me flowers.

God's acceptance of you is your foundation and key for success. Through Him you will recover from all rejection. So look to Him today and trust Christ to turn that rejection around. Something good is coming out of that painful situation. Being accepted by people is not what is important—Being accepted by God is the only thing that really matters.

Many people spend their time and energy trying to be accepted by people who will never accept them. The truth that will set you free is that God has accepted you because of Christ. That fact alone gives you credence as a person.

Rejection does not have to destroy any of us. We must allow rejection to be a stepping stone for our personal growth. I pray that you will allow it to produce growth within you.

At the age of 55 I am a veteran single, and I can tell you that the hurts and rejection of today won't last forever. You won't even remember them after a while. Regarding the guy from Maine, I can't even remember his name or how he looks. The other man—The Player in the House of God—he is one of the ones I wrote my thank you note to at the beginning of this section. As you know, I opened this section up thanking those men who rejected me. I am so glad that I didn't marry any of them. What God has for you will more than make up for those painful days. Keep living and you will live through your present rejection and send a thank you note to those who rejected you as well.

What Do You Do When Your Heart Has Been Broken?

If you have never had your heart broken, you are among the few who can say that. Most of us have experienced some degree of emotional pain. The question before us is not if we shall face emotional pain, but what are you going to do when it comes. How will you cope with pain that can grip your life so tightly that it drains you of your strength and energy? One of the greatest attacks for singles, especially women, is in the area of our emotions. When our hearts have been broken, it is so easy to lose hope and the desire to live.

There are different degrees of emotional pain, just like there are different degrees of physical pain. The problem with emotional pain is that no one can see the bruises on your heart and mind. Sometimes people can be insensitive to the pain you are going through. They make jokes at the most inappropriate times. But you don't want to make them uncomfortable, so you mask your pain. You pretend that all is well, and on a good day you even manage to smile. Your smile hides the fact that they have touched a raw nerve inside of you. Sometimes you are actually dying a little more each day.

If you are like me, you will wait until you find a place of solitude and then let the tears flow freely. Those tears may trickle or come gushing out. When you are alone, you are no longer in fear of being ridiculed or misunderstood.

I have known various degrees of emotional pain. In earlier years I felt I had gone through as much pain as I could handle. I told God I couldn't take any more, but I heard the Lord say, "Don't say that, for you can take some more." His word was true—I have gone through a lot more since that statement, and took some more, more, more, and more...

Whatever the degree of pain you are going through, God can heal you. The songwriter said it well when he wrote, "Earth has no sorrow that heav'n cannot heal. Come to the mercyseat, fervently kneel; here bring your wounded heart, here tell your anguish:" The Psalmist wrote, "The LORD is near to those who have a broken heart, And saves such as have a contrite spirit."

When our heart is aching, we often make the mistake of running to everyone else for advice. Sometimes people will give comforting words; other times their words are as salt poured into an already painful wound. Our first stop when we are experiencing emotional pain should be our prayer closet. Fall on your knees and say like the Psalmist, "Hear my cry, O God; listen to my prayer. From the ends of the earth I call to you, I call as my heart grows faint; lead me to the rock that is higher than I. For you have been my refuge, a strong tower against the foe. I long to dwell in your tent forever and take refuge in the shelter of your wings." (Psalm 61:1-4 (NIV) Psalms 147:3 says, "He heals the brokenhearted and binds up their wound." (NIV) He can make your heart feel cheerful, which will affect your whole life.

You won't always feel instant relief, but you must know by faith He has heard you and will come to your rescue. I can't give you a time schedule when the pain will leave. Every experience is different, but the pain will leave and the tears will dry up. God is faithful and will not leave you in the state of brokenness forever. You must make a conscious decision to place the pain in God's hands and allow Him to heal you and then move on.

Another problem with emotional pain is that sometimes before we can recover completely from one painful situation, we experience another one. It seems so unfair, but God never promised life would be fair. Instead He said, "My grace is sufficient for you." Regardless of how you are feeling, you can make it through whatever pain is in your life.

Keep praying, mediate on God's word, and continue to trust Him. Don't seek for any deep revelations. The important thing is to just draw near to God and get your healing and strength restored. Your prayers do not have to be beautiful words that later can be recorded. There are times I have said, "God, I don't understand this, and I need You to help me. God give me strength." It is not the length of your prayer, but the sincerity and faith exercised within it.

In my first book I described a great heartache I went through; it was called the "Big One". If you want to read about it, buy my book, On the Road to Recovery Again... It is described in Chapter Seven, subsection, Story #2, Prince Charming? I think Not! (pages 109-111).

When people are struggling with agonizing pain—emotional or physical, they need friends who know the importance of just being near. Friends who will lend a listening ear are invaluable. They don't need advice, opinions or sarcasm. Instead they need to know that you care and can empathize with them.

Pain also has it is purpose in our life—it is a crucible that burns away superficiality and our inability to see clearly.

When I went through what I called the "Big One", my faith was tested severely. During that time I was scheduled to do a seminar entitled "Women of Faith Doing the Impossible Through God." I shared with a friend of mine that I wasn't even sure I knew what faith was anymore. I told one of the older mothers about my struggle with faith, and there is no doubt in my mind that they prayed. I not only successfully did a seminar on faith, but I came away with a greater understanding of what faith is.

I thought it would take a long time to get over that pain, but God in His loving grace allowed me to recuperate quickly. But not before He taught me an important lesson. He wanted me to grow up and learn the importance of being grateful in every situation.

There were two Scriptures He gave me to read to emphasize that it is His will for me to be thankful in every situation. The first one was Ephesians 5:20, "Giving thanks always for all things unto God and the Father in the Name of our Lord Jesus Christ." The second one was similar, I Thessalonians 5:18, "In everything give thanks: for this is the will of God in Christ Jesus concerning you." God kept bringing these two passages of Scriptures to my mind continuously.

I did not have a problem with "in everything" give thanks. The word "in" simply is saying regardless of what situation you find yourself in you should give God thanks. That Scripture was easy to digest, but I had a problem with Ephesians 5:20 which says "giving thanks always for all things." How can you give thanks for all things, especially those things that break your heart and make you unhappy?

My limited understanding of the faith walk made me believe that I had stepped out on faith after receiving heaven's approval. I was certain that I had directions to walk this way and was going to become a particular man's bride. I laugh now when I write this, but I felt I had given God plenty of time to act on my behalf. In fact, I also had asked Him if this man was going to marry someone else could He please tell me before it happened.

At first I was all set to say that God didn't tell me before it happened. The truth is this—his wedding plans were announced on national TV, and I received an invitation in the mail. But I didn't accept it and called myself rebuking it. I still believed that God was going to change things. That man married someone else and all my dreams came crashing down. It is amazing how we decide that God has failed us when He doesn't answer the way we think He should.

In my mind I felt God had let me down. Initially I told Him I can't thank you for this right now. I wasn't thankful and didn't appreciate Him allowing me to go through this disappointment. It turned my life upside down and left a dark cloud hanging over my future. The pain I encountered was immeasurable. Discouragement filled my life, and I didn't want to hear anymore messages on faith, vision or prophecy. As far as I was concerned, the principles weren't working. Gwen Wheeler was an angry woman. Life just wasn't making any sense, and I didn't understand why God allowed me to go through this. What was the point?

The whole thing was unfair and basically a waste of my time and faith. Those words were raw, but so real.

You may read this and think how could you dare say those things. Well, many feel and think these same things. I just went a step further and voiced my opinions. In order to be healed, I had to tell God how I was honestly feeling. Besides He already knew, and experience has taught me if I was wrong God would correct me.

At that point I was a desperate woman. God felt so far away from me, and I wasn't going to settle for an indifferent or distant relationship with Him. Being a religious Christian was not my thing; I couldn't be satisfied with just going through the motions. I wanted my intimacy and friendship back with God. The disappointing results made me feel like God had failed me, and this confusion was blocking our flow of communication and fellowship. God doesn't kill people because their desperation causes them to be honest about their feelings. Although at one point death seemed to be a good idea, a safe way out.

Those verses from Ephesians and I Thessalonians kept following me. We were having a wrestling match, and they won. One week later I was finally on my knees. I said, "God, I don't understand why you have allowed me to go through this. I don't have any answers." Yet I reluctantly thanked Him for what had occurred out of obedience to His word. My thank you was not a joyful thank you, but at least I had done what the Bible said. Sometimes you have to just obey even when you don't feel it.

When I said, "thank you", something broke on the inside of me. As time passed by I truly began to feel thankful. I said thank you the next night freer and more joyfully. A transformation happened on the inside of me. My joy and peace came back, and I felt close to

God again. Fourteen years later I am really grateful—grateful he married someone else.

Gratitude is a necessary ingredient in making one whole. Ingratitude is a deadly disease that eats away at us like cancer. It will not only destroy us, but it will separate us from God and other people.

We all have problems, and it is not fun to have painful problems. Yet we must realize that God is bigger than the problem and is present right now in the middle of this painful thing you are going through. When you are experiencing pain, you can still say, Lord, I thank you. I praise you. You are bigger than the pain I am enduring right now, and You are turning it into a blessing! I acknowledge that I have so much to be grateful for. Years later you will discover that there was something you refused to hear or do. God is always faithful and His perspective is eternal compared to your finite limited understanding.

You can choose to focus on the negative or the positive in every situation. Yet it is at the level of praise where God's power can break through in the most dramatic ways and heal you and make you whole.

A spirit of gratitude opens up a doorway to heaven, where a balm or medicine is released into our innermost being. This healing medicine releases us from past hurts, disappointments, insecurities, and guilt.

This healing restoration is a process. It does not happen overnight. Yet it is the spirit of gratitude that sets the healing into motion. With the healing comes the peace of God, which transcends or goes above all human understanding. God's peace will flow into your innermost being, surround you, and will guard your hearts and minds in Christ.

The peace of God cannot be explained or understood. Instead it is to be experienced and enjoyed. All you will know is that I have got peace, restfulness and calmness in the midst of the storm.

Years ago I watched a move about a man who committed suicide because someone he cared about didn't care about him. In fact she walked out of his life. Tears filled my eyes because I knew if it had not been for the grace of God that could have been me. That could have been you.

Yet we are alive today because we have experienced the amazing grace, love and touch of God continuously. He has healed us and will heal us in the future. As the songwriter wrote, "Because He lives I can face tomorrow. Because He lives all fears are gone. Because I know He holds my future and life is worth the living just because He lives." He makes life not only endurable but enjoyable. Another song says, "After all that I have been through, I still have joy!"

Your pain is very real and right now it may be almost unbearable. Yet we have a Savior who not only feels your pain, but He can and will heal that pain. Jesus gave us his reason for coming to earth in Luke 4:18, "The Spirit of the Lord is upon me, because he hath anointed me to preach the gospel to the poor; he hath sent me to heal the brokenhearted, to preach deliverance to the captives, and recovering of sight to the blind, to set at liberty them that are bruised."

Let's pray. Father, in the Name of Jesus, I lift up every person who is suffering from a broken and painful heart. I pray right now that you will release your healing power into their lives. Strengthen, heal and restore them and give them a new vision for their lives. Let not only their hearts be healed but their memory as well. As Isaiah wrote, "Give unto them beauty for ashes, the oil of joy for mourning, the garment of praise for the spirit of heaviness." Amen.

Mark the date down when you read this prayer and accept it as the day that your broken heart was healed. Receive it by faith. Jesus said, "Therefore I tell you, whatever you ask for in prayer, believe that you have received it, and it will be yours." Mark 11:24 (NIV. Sometimes healing is a process and other times it is instantaneous. Just know that today is the day God says, "You are healed!"

In summary, fourteen years later the struggles remain the same:

♥ A Quest for Love

♥ Living Through Loneliness

♥ Coping with Sexuality

♥ Recovering from Rejection

♥ What Do You Do When Your Heart Has Been Broken?

More importantly, our answers and Strength remain the same—God! We will live victorious lives through prayer and fellowship with Him, reading and applying His Word to our lives, and obeying the Holy Spirit's voice. Victory begins today, right now while we are single.

Chapter Six

FOR SINGLE WOMEN ONLY
OVERCOME THE WRONG MAN SYNDROME, PLEASE!

There is a syndrome that has made so many women's lives miserable. It has caused so much pain and frustration. That syndrome is called the "Wrong Man Syndrome"—better known as desperation. The "Wrong Man Syndrome" means marrying the wrong man because you are afraid you might not get another chance at marriage. You don't want to spend another night alone, so you opt to marry the wrong man simply because he asked you. But marriage is not a cure for loneliness. Just ask some married women. Some of their husbands lie beside them every night, but they are still lonely. I remember years ago discussing how lonely single women get, and a couple of married women in our group spoke up and said, "We are lonely too." That statement shocked me; they shattered my Cinderella thinking that marriage always meant living "happily ever after."

Unfortunately, the church has become a place where this syndrome is allowed to incubate. Most women in the church have been indoctrinated all of their lives about the importance of becoming somebody's wife. So after a certain time passes and they are not married, they get anxious and sometimes very desperate. The "Wrong Man Syndrome" starts penetrating into their veins. They treat singleness as a disease to be cured or a misfortune to recover from.

It's time to stop fantasying about "Mr. Right" coming into your life to rescue you from your tower of gloom and misery. Don't see every single man in the church as potential mates; see them as your brother and they may become your friends. If you develop a romantic relationship as a result of that friendship, don't ignore obvious warning signs. Someone said that the seeds of divorce are sown before marriage.

Furthermore, don't assume that because a man is saved and goes to church that he is a good marriage candidate. In case you don't know, the church is not a place for the perfect. But it is a maturing laboratory where we receive the Word of God and fellowship so that we can go on to perfection. Many people are still in the process of growing up and have unripe fruit. That fruit needs to ripen before they are ready to marry anyone.

You say, "He's got a good job, house, and he can take care of me." I am glad to hear that, but my question to you is: how is he going to treat you when he is away from the church behind closed doors? Too many men who confess to be Christians are abusing women. The sad fact is that women see violent behavioral patterns during courtship, but convince themselves or allow others to convince them that things will work out.

Don't be blinded by a man's title or his position within the church. Women mistakenly believe that every man in a leadership role in churches is mature. The maturity of a man is often measured by his titles: ordained minister, deacon, Sunday school teacher, youth pastor, president of the men's ministry, evangelist or the pastor's right hand man. You say he operates in all nine of the spiritual gifts. You ask me, "Are you impressed?" No, I am not impressed.

For Jesus said: "Beware of false prophets, which come to you in sheep's clothing, but inwardly they are ravening wolves. Ye shall know them by their fruits. Do men gather grapes of thorns, or figs of thistles? Even so every good tree bringeth forth good fruit; but a corrupt tree bringeth forth evil fruit. A good tree cannot bring forth evil fruit, neither can a corrupt tree bring forth good fruit." The fruit is the character; look for character not for positions or titles.

Also, God should always be your greatest advisor in this. How much peace do you have about marrying that person? God is not the author of confusion, and enduring a bad marriage is not suffering for the sake of Christ. Yes, you do deserve better. In fact you deserve the best! Your past mistakes do not nullify your future in God. God does not ordain bad marriages to perfect us. He has plenty of other methods that He uses.

Believe it or not, your husband may be sitting somewhere in the church that you attend, but God has him hidden. He may not be ready for you, for he is a diamond in the rough, a miracle in the making, and a possibility that is just about to happen. God is getting ready to release him into his destiny. So don't be discouraged because he does not hold a position in the church. Instead, praise God that he is a good, hardworking, and saved man. He may not have prestige or recognition, but more importantly, he has character. From the surface you can't see the treasure God has invested in him. Yet God sees the real person on the inside, and He knows how well that man will fit into your life.

On the other hand, you may think you know who he is, and you may be right. Because he is not moving as quickly as you think he should, you may be tempted to make the first move. I have one word for you—Don't! Proverbs 18:22 tells us, "The man who finds a wife

finds a treasure and receives favor from the LORD."
(NLT)

God's design for marriage is that man is to be the
pursuer and woman the pursued. I don't believe that
there is only one person you can be married to—God
gives us options. Both wills have to line up with each
other. As you will agree, typically men have more
options than women do. Sometimes he may be praying
about two available options. You may be the better
choice, but because you made the first move, he
decided on the other option. There is something within
a normal man's makeup that says I want to make the
first move. Don't get angry with God because He didn't
make this man marry you. Accept the fact that you
violated the rules and nullified the plans. So move on.

I attended a family conference years ago. The speaker
was a man and said, "A man's greatest fear is to be
controlled by a woman." Men need to be in the lead
role of initiating a marital relationship. I could go into
greater details about the mistake of making the first
move, but I won't. Just trust me when I say, I've been
there and done that, and don't want to go that way no
more. The results were very painful, and I advise you
not to do it. Learn from my mistakes.

Rest in God, and don't make the mistake of comparing
your notes with other women. Each woman must walk
her own personal walk, and God will grant us the grace
to complete our stories. There is a reason why you are
waiting longer than someone else. I believe the
stronger a woman's will is the longer her wait will be.
The average man can't handle our strength and
complex personalities. My older brother once told me
that. We don't fit into their blueprint of the way a wife
should be. Our uniqueness is apparent—we know that
we are different. God has to send our husbands

through a special school of training in order to prepare him for us.

At one time I felt bad about being me, and even cried about it. It seemed as though most men were scared off, especially as I got older. I admit that because of the ministry I don't focus a lot on the idea of being "Miss Susie Homemaker." Cooking, organizing, and cleaning are tasks I perform well. But I would rather be writing, traveling the world preaching the gospel and conducting workshops. That doesn't make me a bad person. I just don't fit into the "normal wife" category. So at my age I have to accept those facts about myself, and I know that marrying the wrong man would destroy my destiny.

One of the biggest mistakes women can make is to get married before they find out who they are. A man marries you on the basis that you fit into the "normal wife" category. When you start growing up and sense a greater call on your life, you think your husband should understand. But most men don't; they want the woman they married to stay the woman they married. They are not interested in being married to the woman you are emerging to be. If you are already married and going through this transition, I can't give you advice on that one. You need another counselor to tell you what to do.

But for those of you, who are still living in the "waiting zone," take courage in the words of this Scripture, "And let us not be weary in well doing: for in due season we shall reap, if we faint not."

Please don't settle for anyone less than the man God has ordained for you. Somebody reading this may have to adjust your wedding plans. Yes, I understand that the invitations have been sent out; the gown is bought; the caterer has been paid-in-full. The out-of-town relatives have bought their plane tickets. A change in plans would be a great inconvenience for everyone, but a lifetime of being married to the wrong man will be a greater inconvenience. Your family may thank you later for not having to see him at every family gathering. Just think about your own mental, emotional, and physical wellbeing. You may suffer humiliation right now, but you could be avoiding a greater one in the future.

Pay attention to the warning signals. Are they blinking off and on like a neon light? Are they saying: Don't do this! Hear God's voice! God will grant you the grace to adjust your vision and life. You may be thinking, "You don't understand; I am in love with him, or I am 45 plus years old, and I may not get another chance for happiness." If this is a mistake, this is not a chance for happiness. This is a choice for misery. It really is ok to be single after 40 or 50. I am 55 years old and I have no regrets.

In fact, when I think about a man I could have gotten married to 23 years ago, I am just so grateful that I obeyed the voice of God and didn't marry him. I know what it feels like to tell a man you are in love with that you can't marry him because God said no.

Here's my story... I fell in love quickly for the first time when I was 22 years old. For this writing I will call this man Barry. It's not necessary that you know his real name; he is deceased. I was invited to a service to hear Barry preach. After service we were introduced to each other, and there was an instant attraction between the two of us.

After it was confirmed that there was a mutual interest, we started seeing each other. Barry had all the outward markings of a successful man: he was handsome, well dressed, intelligent, a Pentecostal ordained minister, and had high goals. Also, he had a lot of class and was fun to be with. We went to the theater to see plays and also to amusement parks. At first he didn't have much money because he was in college. Later on he became successful in Corporate America.

As a matter of fact, he was very ambitious and climbed the corporate ladder quickly even before finishing college. He enrolled into an accelerated management program, which required him to travel a lot. During one of those absences God told me he was not the one for me to marry. As I was riding on the subway, I heard the word, no, ringing down in my spirit. I didn't have to ask what it meant. God had communicated to me in such a way that I knew He was telling me I wasn't to marry Barry. Immediately I wrote Barry a letter and told him what God had said. At that time, it wasn't hard to write that letter because it was not the best time in our relationship. By that time negative fruits and character flaws were in full bloom in his life. He was arrogant, self-centered, aloof, cold, effeminate, and insensitive. I welcomed a relief from this whole situation.

A few years later I went through a time of confusion. I was disappointed in another relationship, and because Barry was still calling me, I thought maybe God didn't really say no. He invited me to visit him, but I was still struggling with whether or not he was gay. There were enough signs that I saw and heard, but I was in denial. I decided to write him a letter. Within the letter I told him the reason my brothers didn't want us to get married: they thought he was gay. I assured him I defended him. He never responded to that letter, instead he called and said he hadn't heard from me. The nervousness and hesitation in his voice indicated that he had indeed received the letter. By not denying his gay lifestyle, he was admitting to it. When I got off the phone, I was angry because I felt he should have been honest. He was denying me the right to choose whether or not I wanted to be married to a gay man. That was my choice alone. But I never mentioned it again—I just knew I was not going to marry him.

After some considerable time had passed, I received a call from Barry. Ten years had passed since we first met; he was 30 and I was 32. He felt he was ready to get married, and I was still the one he wanted to marry. I don't know what his criteria for marriage were. Maybe he just wanted to be with the person who fell in love with him before he became successful. He always feared that a woman would marry him only for what he had and not for himself.

His proposal that day was unique but not in a positive way. In fact, I thought he was just joking. He said, "I have three candidates for marriage, and you are candidate #1, will you marry me?" I laughed at first, because I didn't think he was serious. How could he be? His approach was the zenith of arrogance. When I realized he was serious, I seriously said no. He couldn't believe I was turning him down. God's word to me was plain: I was not to marry him.

I felt good that I was able to stand my ground. But then Satan began to try and shake that ground by telling me I deserved to share in this man's success. Here was my opportunity to reap the rewards of the struggles of the past. I had been with him during his struggling days in college, and should have something to show for it. He interjected thoughts about the house that Barry owned, and wanted me to see myself living in it.

Barry called a couple of weeks later to say he was getting married. I don't know if he chose candidate #2 or #3. It didn't matter. A divine mandate came from God that I was not to marry this man. My greatest test occurred when Barry came to a revival I was ministering at. It was the final night. My sermon was about abundant living. I was at the height of my sermon when he walked through the doors. His unexpected appearance caused a jolt to occur in my message. But by the grace of God I was able to regain my composure and finished my sermon.

It had been four months since we spoke on the phone about marriage and years since I last saw him in person. All the love I thought had faded away rose up inside of me. We went out to eat after service. He said my facial expressions communicated to him that I wished I had said yes. Then he asked me an agonizing question: "Did you change your mind?" My answer was no. I assured him it wasn't because I didn't love him. The reason was because God said no, and I couldn't go beyond the word of God. That explanation seemed to finally satisfy him. He knew he was up against a power that he could not manipulate.

That Sunday when I went to church I was hurting so much that I didn't know how I would make it through the day. Then I looked up at a sign on the church's wall which read, "I am the Lord that healeth thee."

The next day my friend, Doris, called from Illinois. I told her what had happened, and asked her why God was allowing this to happen. She said, "Gwen, you know all the facts, and God wants you to weigh all the facts and make a conscious decision."

Then the Holy Spirit brought to mind the words written in Hebrews 11:24-26:

"By faith Moses, when he became of age, refused to be called the son of Pharaoh's daughter, choosing rather to suffer affliction with the people of God than to enjoy the passing pleasures of sin, esteeming the reproach of Christ greater riches than the treasure in Egypt; For he looked to the reward."

Obedience is a choice. Nothing worthwhile in life comes without some pain. I made up my mind that day to obey God, and I knew that my choice was forever settled in heaven. It hurt to read his wedding invitation, and it hurt to know he actually married someone else.

At first God did not give me a reason why I could not marry him. The fact that He said no was the only reason I needed. After Barry was married, God showed me a dream that confirmed Barry was gay.

For years I lived with the feeling that I would receive a call that Barry had died. That feeling became a reality about eight years after he was married. The first call came that he was dying. A second call came two days later, and I was told that he had died. I didn't speak to the medical examiner, but all the signs indicated that he died from AIDS.

I am grateful that I listened and obeyed the voice of God. My prayer is that you will listen and obey too. How different my life would be if I had not obeyed God. I might not be alive and writing this chapter to you. Whenever God says no, there is a reason. Your circumstances may be completely different from mine; they may not be as dramatic. The man who wants to marry you may be truly saved and a wonderful man of God, but to marry him means death to your destiny. It means being out of the will of God. Every woman is not the same; your destiny is not like your girlfriend's destiny. Stop comparing yourself to her and feeling that life is passing you by. Please don't think that you have to jump on the marriage train at any cost.

I wrote a poems addressing this issue *entitled **When God Says No About The Person You Love.***

When God Says No About The Person You Love

By Gwendolyn J. Wheeler

You have fallen in love, but you didn't plan it that way,

So you have decided to be with that person always.

Yet you realized the future is not yours alone to plan,
So asked for God's will regarding marrying that man.
You fell on your knees in humility to seek God's will,
Believing He would say yes, and your desire fulfill.
But to your surprise He said that man is not the one,
And now you're struggling to say, "thy will be done."
Your eyes are filled with tears and your heart is in pain;
You're wondering if your prayers were prayed in vain.
That person seems to match the blueprint in your mind,
Another person like him would be so hard to find.
Surely God must understand the love in your heart,
And how much it would hurt you, if you had to depart.
God doesn't get a thrill out of saying no to you;
But you are human and have a very limited view.
You can see only today, whereas God sees tomorrow,
He knows if you marry that man you'll end up in sorrow.
I've been where you are and know how you feel;
Please take my advice and submit to God's will.
I was deeply in love many years ago;
It hurt me too when God told me no.
I made the choice that day to trust and to obey;
I am glad that I did and have no regrets today.
I have lived long enough to understand and see,
Why God said no, that man wasn't for me.
Don't make the mistake and disobey God's voice,
And marry that person you consider your choice.

90

Everything that glitters certainly isn't real gold,

And if you dare to wait a better vision will unfold.

A vision of peace, joy, healing, wealth, and much happiness,

When you marry God's choice and experience marital bliss.

In conclusion, my dear sister, be whole, be happy, and be content. Don't fall victim to the Wrong Man Syndrome.

Chapter Seven

Wedding Bell Blues? I Think Not!

Like most young girls of my era, I grew up believing and dreaming I would be a young bride. I wanted to be married and have my children by the age of 30. But my story didn't unfold that way. At this writing I am 55 (2009), single and because of surgery I am not able to have children. If I hadn't had the surgery, at 55 I have lost the desire to have any.

Within my life I have experienced varying emotions about being single. I have known depression, dissatisfaction, loneliness, and I am sure desperation. At other times, I have been patient, content, hopeful, and peaceful. Because of God's grace, I am now experiencing the later four positive emotions.

How can a 55-year-old woman be at peace about being single, and not be experiencing the "wedding bells blues"? The number one reason is God. He has developed peace within my heart and taught me how to live successfully as a single person. I believe the season is near for marriage, but as my poem declares: while I am waiting, I don't have to be blue. There are tasks to be finished. Solomon wrote: "To everything there is a season." Some seasons are longer than others are, and this has been a long but fruitful season.

Having God in my life is more important than the promise of marriage. He continues to be my greatest Source of peace, joy, contentment and happiness. His love for me is better than life.

It takes a long time for God to work some things out in our lives, and you have to be willing to wait—sometimes many years. I received the following letter from a friend of mine named Willie Etta Wright in 1988. When I received it, I was 34 years old—21years ago. Willie, can you believe I am still holding onto your words? Here are the words from her letter:

"Being single and being willing to wait on the Lord is a rewarding experience. It's rewarding because you are leaning on Him and flourishing because of His promises. It's a great realm in which to be. Even though I have a husband, my experiences as a single woman have made me the woman that I am today. It does pay to wait on the Lord. Relish all the lessons that the Lord teaches you while you are single, for when He blesses you with that special person you will need to draw upon those lessons. I believe that that special person is coming for you. Don't get faint. Don't get weary! Hold on! Be of good courage! That person is tailor made for you. He has already been prepared for you. From somewhere he's coming. Some time will be your time."

A second letter came soon after that.

"Be of good courage! If God can bless me with a husband, He can bless you. God doesn't have just anybody waiting in the wings for you. Don't faint in your waiting. The wait is well worth it. Many times I wondered why the Lord had me to wait for so long. There was a reason. I had to grow in my experiences with God. I learned how to lean on Jesus. These learnings have been invaluable in my life now.

Your time and change will come in God's own time. Wait on Him! You don't want to rush to get someone who will make your life miserable. You

***deserve to have a wonderful future with God's
man."***

Willie was 41 years old when she got married and I can
still see her in her wedding gown, and hearing her say
these words, "Single women, don't give up!" Thanks,
Willie, I haven't given up.

The years have unveiled many important facts to me,
and allowed me to understand why God said no about
some of the men I wanted to marry. When I discovered
how their lives have turned out, I said thank You, Lord,
for not allowing me to marry them.

In my book, One is a Whole Number, I wrote about how
to handle heartbreak, heartache and emotional pain. In
order to help my readers understand the different
degrees of pain, I referred to the "Big One". I wrote
about the effects of this. My words were: "Emotionally I
felt I had been thrown against a brick wall and had
been shattered into many pieces. I felt betrayed and
rejected.

I kept trying to hold onto faith, but when the unexpected
occurred I found myself crying many more days. I have
experienced what David wrote when he said, "My tears
have been my meat both night and day." I went to bed
crying and I woke up crying. I sat in church with tears
rolling down my face.

When confirmation was given that the event I dreaded
occurred, I pulled the covers over my head, wishing I
wouldn't have to face the next day. I longed for death.
Then I heard the Lord say, "oh yeah?" He nursed me
and rocked me through the night. That was one of the
longest nights in my life. He immediately began to
minister to me that things weren't really as they
seemed."

The details of what the "Big One" represented was
purposely left out. I was too embarrassed to admit that

94

my pain occurred because a man I thought I was going to marry—married someone else. Today I am no longer embarrassed to admit to that fact. That part of my life is over, and I am better because of the experience.

Thankfully I emerged out of that situation a stronger and whole woman. The title of my first book, <u>One is a Whole Number</u>, was birthed out of that painful situation. God taught me that as a single person I am a whole person and do not need anyone else to make me complete.

In time a greater sense of purpose and destiny was birthed into my life. I am a pastor/teacher with a prophetic and evangelistic anointing, a published author, workshop leader, mentor, worship leader, a business woman, and an entrepreneur. Two additional ministries have been birthed: Gwen Wheeler International Ministries and It is Possible International Outreach Ministries.

After Mr. Right married who he considered to be Ms. Right, I felt like dying. I am so grateful that I kept on living, recovered, and discovered the woman of destiny that God purposed me to be. Marriage is in my future, but I am not depending on Mr. Right to make me Miss Right. I am Miss Right all by myself. To God be the glory! The following poem, *A Celebration of My Life,* was also birthed out of that painful situation.

A Celebration of My Life

By Gwendolyn J. Wheeler

I started out shy, withdrawn, lacking confidence and self-esteem,

Didn't know who I was, or what goal I was in this world to achieve.

Then I found God, His love and sensed a great purpose for my life;

I dreamed untraditional dreams, and wanted to be more than just a wife.

Young girls were taught to be feminine, to cook and to clean,

Yet thoughts of achieving greatness filled my every dream.

There has to be more in life than just being a man's wife;

I want to preach, create, analyze, and build a successful life.

I want to excel, lead, be strong, and to myself be true;

I must be strong when others criticize my point of view.

My dreams of greatness collided with another dream of mine,

A dream to marry Mr. Right, believing happiness I would find.

I dreamed of someone strong, who would desire to be the best,

Who would share my life of greatness and excel above the rest.

I thought I found someone, who fitted the description above;

I believed he would gladly marry me and share a lasting love.

But my dream to marry Mr. Right was really a mere fantasy,

This man wasn't the person I thought or imagined him to be.

I made the mistake of admiring him because I considered him great,

Only to be rejected and experienced a tremendous heartbreak.

I found out later amidst the ashes of much disappointment and pain,

He didn't want an anointed woman who would the gospel proclaim.

He wanted a pretty woman, who would only smile and look good,

Not one who would excel, stand strong, and be the best she could.

I screamed and I cried through so many days and endless nights,

And wondered if I would win this long, painful, and emotional fight.

I struggled with my identity and for a brief moment I felt like dying,

But by the grace of God I regrouped and stopped my constant crying.

I reexamined myself, my dreams, and who I really wanted to be,

And through this examination I realized I had the right to be me.

So today I celebrate my life, my choice, and my successful dreams;

I am reaching for greatness though difficult the path sometimes seem.

Some days we experience so much pain when we are rejected; we think that is the worst thing that could happen to us. I thought the "Big One" (definition of my heartbreak in 1994) was the worst thing that could happen to me. Then I lost my two brothers, Thaddeus and Sherwin in 1997. Their deaths were five months apart. (details recorded in my book, <u>On the Road to Recovery Again...</u>) Two years later, 1999, I lost one of the greatest cheerleaders in my life, my grandmother, Gaynell Terrell. Each loss was different but very painful; yes, worse than the pain I experienced with the "Big One". Whatever pain I experienced with the "Big One" is a distant memory; it's like a bad dream I woke up from.

Emotional pain comes in so many other ways. Another life-changing event occurred in October 2005. A few months after my book, <u>On the Road to Recovery...</u>, was released, my mother suffered a stroke. I am grateful that she is still here and recovered at home for a while. Watching your mother recover from a stroke is also a type of loss. I have lost part of my mother that may never be recovered. Changes have taken place in her body and mind. Parts of the friendship and life resource have been fractured by the stroke. We can't interact fully in the way we once did and I miss that. Strokes just rob people of part of their perception.

Emotional pain will always come in varying degrees, but you don't have to live in constant misery because you are single. If the wedding bells never ring in your life, you owe it to yourself to be happy. Remember this and smile: If you marry Mr. or Miss Wrong, you will really have the wedding bell blues—the type that isn't easy to cure.

As one of your life coaches, I am cheering you on to live your best life now. Be whole, be happy, and discover the exciting, single you that is waiting to emerge on life's soil. The world is waiting to applaud that emergence.

Marriage—Pursue or Release?

Below are some edited excerpts from my first book, <u>One Is a Whole Number.</u>

Before we ponder the question, should we get married, we must understand who we are and what God has called us to do. You don't want to be married to someone who does not respect the call of God on your life or the career path you have chosen to take. At first it may seem worth the sacrifice, but later you will resent that person. You will feel they have robed you of your God-given rights. Therefore, honesty is necessary in any relationship. Please don't consider marriage until you first find out who you are.

Also, everyone will not get married. This section of my book is not intended to convey the message that if you ask God for a husband or a wife you will get one. I don't know God's plan for your life and will not try and interpret how God will respond to your request.

This section is to encourage you to seek God's will for your life. Proverbs 3:6 says: "In all your ways acknowledge Him, and He shall direct your paths." Psalms 37:23 declares "The steps of a good man are ordered by the Lord, and He delights in his way."

If God says marriage is part of the plan He has for your life, then prepare yourself first and then pursue it. Begin by becoming a whole, successful single person. I hope this book has helped you to make some positive steps toward living a whole, successful single life.

If He says singleness is your life's journey, then find out how you can release your desire to be married into His hands. Find out how you can creatively live your life.

When God says no about a request, He gives you the grace to accept the no and in time will reveal to you the better plan for your life. I say better because God is not in the business of giving His children second rate plans, but He gives us the best plans for our lives regardless of how it may look on the outside.

Relinquishment is not an easy process. It may take months or even years. Therefore, we must be careful not to allow the root of bitterness to grow in our hearts. Bitterness will rob you of the joy and peace that God gives to those who will dare to live out His plan for their lives.

God's reasons for allowing us to be single are sometimes too difficult for us to understand right away. We may not always be given a reason but just the grace to live our lives one day at a time. If we will trust Him, we will be able to look back and realize the positive things that our singleness has brought about.

Some may feel life has dealt you a bad card, while others may say the right person hasn't come along and may not come along. There are others who feel they are not attractive enough—e.g., too fat, too skinny, mediocre facial characteristics, too short, or too tall. Still others feel you are too old, or too poor. Hopefully, there are others who know that they are single at this time because it is God's perfect will.

Outside circumstances do not influence God when He is making a decision about your life. God doesn't give out husbands or wives based on how pretty or handsome you are. It doesn't matter if you are intelligent or rich. God looks at the heart. He sees our dedication, faith, dreams, our level of commitment, weaknesses and strengths. He then weighs them out in relationship to His plan and purpose for our lives. These facts are what He uses to determine if marriage is the best route for us to go.

Like the Psalmist you can say: "Morning by morning, O Lord, you hear my voice; morning by morning I lay my requests before you and wait in expectation!" You can expect God to communicate the answers to us in various ways. He may speak to our hearts through an inner voice, which can be in the form of words or just an inner knowing. Other times He confirms through His Word or through other people. Yet whatever answer you think you have gotten, make sure it is accompanied by inner peace. God is not the author of confusion. Even when His will does not agree with what you want, there should be a prevailing peace that will pervade your heart. Make sure you know for yourself. Don't just take another person's word or opinion. People can be right about one situation and wrong about something us.

I am reminded about a woman God used to encourage me many years ago. She spoke a word to me that was right on the money; she didn't even know me. This occurred in a different state then where I lived. The next time I went there she gave me another prophecy. Because she was right the first time, I didn't think she could be wrong this time. She told me that I was going to get married. Her words went something like this: "You will have your diamond by Christmas and be married by April." Those dates passed by and neither events occurred. When I saw her the next time she said, "What happened? I know I heard from God. Sometimes we don't want to marry who God has for us." I smiled at her because I knew she had missed the mark. The only person that had been in my life since that prophecy was a "down low" brother and God plainly spoke to me that he wasn't the person I should marry. (Details about him are given in the Chapter entitled, "The Wrong Man Syndrome")

God is faithful and will speak to you on whatever level you can understand. Be sure to allow Him the time and space to speak to you.

If we receive a yes from God regarding marriage, there may be many years of waiting as God prepares us to take this big step in our lives. Very few realize the importance of preparation for marriage. We prepare for our careers and ministries, but fail to see the importance of preparing to share our lives with another person. There are issues in our lives that need to be resolved before we can adequately relate to another person within marriage.

Oftentimes problems in marriages began while people were single. Because they did not resolve those issues while they were single, they are now forced to deal with them in marriages. So many of us have false ideas and expectations and need help in distinguishing between reality and fantasy. We do not need to force others to try and live up to those impossible expectations.

People who emphasize the importance of getting married don't always provide advice to singles on how to prepare themselves for marriage—i.e. ,how to pray to God and receive an answer as to whether marriage is part of His plan for their lives, or how to know when it is the right time and/or right person.

It disturbs me when I hear of young singles as well as older singles who marry people who are obviously not right for them. Sometimes the warning signals are flashing like neon lights telling them to stop—don't marry him or her. You will be sorry if you do. But they just run right pass those warning signals, feeling this may be their only chance for marriage.

So many are willing to marry the wrong person just to avoid being single. They treat being single as though it is a dreaded disease to be cured. Yet it is a gift that God has so graciously granted to us.

Your singleness may be temporary or permanent. My advice is to find out what God is saying to you. If there are some mature Christians in your life, who you know can be trusted, have them pray with you. Just one thing—be sure you really want to know God's will for you.

Regardless of the answer you receive, be happy, be content, take your life off hold and live it to the fullest! Be a whole, successful single person.

Chapter Eight

Conclusion—Where Do We Go From Here?

So where do we go from here? If you are a successful single person, continue on your journey—complete your mission. There are various levels of wholeness and success, and none of us will graduate from this school of learning until we are in heaven. How shall we look when we become totally whole? John said it well when he wrote in I John 3:2, "Beloved, now we are children of God; and it has not yet been revealed what we shall be, but we know that when He is revealed, we shall be like Him, for we shall see Him as He is." There is no higher level of wholeness than this. Paul added to this in Ephesians 4:13, "till we all come to the unity of the faith and of the knowledge of the Son of God, to a perfect man, to the measure of the stature of the fullness of Christ."

You can't figure out if you are successful? Re-read this book and underline those principles that apply to the areas you are struggling with. Don't give up on yourself. Being a successful single person is a journey towards wholeness and wholeness is a process. You must remember those words or else you will be frustrated and discouraged, especially on those days when it seems you are losing the battles. Patience and perseverance are necessary virtues if you expect to arrive at the state of wholeness and success.

For those of you who are sure that you are not successful, the above paragraph applies to you as well. Don't give up! Set your face towards wholeness and success. Don't allow your past failures or disappointments to hold you back. Today is a brand new day and opportunity to become what God has called you to be—a whole, successful individual. You must believe in your heart that wholeness and success are possible for you now while you are single.

Some of you may want to respond like Mary did in the book of Luke and say, "How can this be, since..." She gave her reasons why she didn't think what the angel said could become possible. You too may have your excuses/reasons, but let's remember the angel's response to Mary, "For with God nothing will be impossible."

Take your eyes off yourself and your failures. Look to God! He hasn't given up on you and doesn't want you to give up on yourself. Always remember that God is the essential ingredient for wholeness and success. Don't look to anyone or anything else or failure and disappointments will be the prizes you will gain.

I am sure if you examine your life closer, you are more successful than you think you are. What we oftentimes consider failures are actually learning opportunities. Instead of beating yourself up, ask yourself the question, what can I learn from this? Then do what I said to do in Chapter One of this book. I encouraged everyone to celebrate. Let me repeat some of the words I wrote:

My single years are to be commemorated. Yes, I have had my struggles: the loneliness, the sexual temptations (some fiercer than others), the desperation, the wrong choices, betrayals, failures, rejections, heartbreak/heartache, and the "wrong man syndrome". Certainly, I have asked the question, why am I still single, God? That has haunted me, but not for long. God has always comforted me.

Mid-life is here—no place for regrets or self-pity. I am here now. Fifty-five—how did I reach this age so soon? With midlife come changes in my health—high blood pressure, less energy, aches and pains in every part of my body. The body doesn't work like it used to, but thank God I am alive. Every day I wake up and can get up out of bed is a reason to celebrate.

A post note: It has been a few months since I wrote the above paragraph regarding midlife changes. It is easy to attribute failing health to our aging bodies. But the truth is this—we can slow down our ageing and rid our bodies from some of our illnesses by changing the way we eat and exercise more.

I have tried to address every issue I felt pertinent to the single. If I have forgotten something important, remember God has already provided the solution you need. Go to Him with every problem and concern that you have.

Remember the words found in Hebrews 4:15-16,

"For we do not have a High Priest who cannot sympathize with our weaknesses, but was in all points tempted as we are, yet without sin. Let us therefore come boldly to the throne of grace, that we may obtain mercy and find grace to help in time of need."

Do you have needs today? God's grace continues to be sufficient to help. We can go to Him when we can't go to anyone else. You can find help at the throne of God. Just admit your need. Don't try and cover it up. Take off your mask and confess your deepest longings to Him. I close with the words of a song that has comforted me a many a day.

"I must tell Jesus all of my trials, I cannot bear these burdens alone; In my distress He kindly will help me, He always loves and cares for His own. I must tell

Jesus! I must tell Jesus! I cannot bear my burdens alone: I must tell Jesus! Jesus can help me, Jesus alone."

Yes, sometimes the struggles of being single may seem like burdens too difficult to carry, but Jesus can and will help you, Jesus alone.

God bless you! Now go forward in your successful single living. A whole new world is waiting for you.

To order Additional Copies of
One is Still A Whole Number
or *On the Road to Recovery Again...*

You may order three ways:

Checks or Money Orders
Use the order blank below and send to:

Gwen Wheeler International Ministries, Inc. (GWIM)
P. O. Box 2852
Lynn, MA 01903

Make out checks or money orders to GWIM.

Credit Card orders
Call Gwen Wheeler at 781-771-5399. Have your credit card ready.

You may also order through Infinity Publishing's website, www.bbotw.com.

Order Blank
Name _____

Address _____

City _____ State _____

Zip code _____

One is Still A Whole Number			
Quantity	Unit Price	Tax & Shipping	Total Amount
	12.95	$3.55 (1st book) $1.00 per additional book	

On the Road to Recovery Again...			
Quantity	Unit Price	Tax & Shipping	Total Amount
	$15.95	$4.00 (1st book) $1.00 per additional book	

Contact the Author

➢ Bookings for retreats, conferences, workshops, empowerment/motivational sessions, and seminars—write:

Gwen Wheeler International Ministries, Inc.
P. O. Box 2852
Lynn, MA 01903

Via e-mail—revgwen@comcast.net

Or you may call 781-598- 1278

If you live in Massachusetts and want to order flowers, contact me at **Sensational Flower Designs By Gwendolyn**, 781-771-5399 or gwenfloral@yahoo.com. The website is presently being constructed.